ACC NO: TO1675
AUTHOR: HARTLEY
RECEIVED: 6/7/09
SECTION: HM 141 HAR

D1464318

PLACING

LADDERS

This book is due for return on or before the last date shown below.

24. AUG. 2009

11/9

12 APR. 2010

-4. FEB. 2011

12. MAY 2011

24. OCT. 2011

21·11·11

-2. JAN. 2013

11/5/21

19. DEC 2013

Centre Library

675

PLACING LADDERS

HARNESSING OUR LEADERSHIP POTENTIAL

Julian Hartley & Anthony Bell
(eds)

a co-publication

 **Kingsham Press**
www.akdpress.com

 NHS NORTH WEST
LEADERSHIP ACADEMY

First published in 2009
by Kingsham Press and NHS North West Leadership Academy

Kingsham Press
Oldbury Complex
Marsh Lane
Easthampnett
Chichester, West Sussex
PO18 0JW

NHS North West Leadership Academy
Gateway House
Manchester
M60 7LP

© 2009, Julian Hartley; Anthony Bell
© 2009, Deborah Chafer (Chapter 1); Anthony Bell (Chapter 2); Phil Morley
(Chapter 3); Judith Griffin (Chapter 4); Caroline Shaw (Chapter 5); Leigh Griffin
(Chapter 6); David Fillingham, CBE (Chapter 7); Stephen Dalton (Chapter 8);
James Birrell (Chapter 9); Anita Marsland, MBE (Chapter 10); Sheena Cumiskey
(Chapter 11); Derek Campbell (Chapter 12); Julian Hartley (Chapter 13);
Ian Cumming, OBE (Chapter 14); Simon Barber (Chapter 15); Mike Burrows
(Chapter 16)

Typeset in Garamond

Printed and bound in the UK

ISBN: 978-1-904235-65-1

All rights reserved. No part of this book may be reprinted or reproduced or
utilised in any form or by any electronic, mechanical, or other means, now
known or later invented, including photocopying and recording, or in any
information storage or retrieval system, without the prior permission in writing
from the publishers.

British Library Cataloging in Publication Data
A catalogue record of this book is available from the British Library

Hartley, Julian; Bell, Anthony

ACKNOWLEDGEMENTS

Placing Ladders: harnessing our leadership potential has been made possible by the foresight of Deborah Chafer and Deborah Arnot at the NHS North West Leadership Academy. In addition gratitude is expressed to the 15 Chief Executives for making time from their busy schedules to share their stories, experiences and insights.

A number of colleagues have also been supportive during the production stage of the publication. Alicia Custis, Jane Raven and Val Wormald have provided much help and encouragement in moving the publication along.

The Contributors of Chapters 4 and 11 and the Publishers gratefully acknowledge the use of extracts of the Leadership Qualities Framework. A shorter version of Anthony Bell's story was first published on line by the Health Foundation. Extracts in Ian Cumming's Chapter was earlier published in The Little Black Book of Leadership hints and tips for healthcare staff by NHS North Lancashire.

Finally the publication would not have happened in so timely a fashion without the expert technical help from Marie Doherty.

ABOUT THE CONTRIBUTORS

Deborah Chafer is Director of the NHS North West Leadership Academy and was formerly Associate Director of Organisational Development at NHS North West.

Anthony Bell is Chief Executive of the Royal Liverpool and Broadgreen University Hospitals NHS Trust.

Phil Morley is Chief Executive of Mid-Cheshire Hospitals NHS Foundation Trust.

Judith Griffin is Chief Executive of Blackburn with Darwen Teaching Primary Care Trust.

Caroline Shaw is Chief Executive of Christie Hospital NHS Foundation Trust.

Dr Leigh Griffin is Chief Executive of Sefton Primary Care Trust.

David Fillingham, CBE is Chief Executive of Bolton Hospitals NHS Foundation Trust.

Stephen Dalton is Chief Executive of Cumbria Partnership NHS Foundation Trust.

James Birrell is Chief Executive of Aintree University Hospitals NHS Foundation Trust.

Anita Marsland, MBE is Chief Executive of Knowsley Health & Wellbeing.

Sheena Cumiskey is Chief Executive of Trafford Primary Care Trust.

Derek Campbell is Chief Executive of Liverpool Primary Care Trust.

Julian Hartley is Chief Executive of Blackpool, Fylde & Wyre Hospitals Foundation Trust.

Ian Cumming, OBE is Chief Executive of North Lancashire Teaching Primary Care Trust.

Simon Barber is Chief Executive of 5 Boroughs Partnership NHS Trust.

Dr Mike Burrows is Chief Executive of Salford Primary Care Trust.

CONTENTS

FOREWORD

Mike Farrar, CBE

I know that you will agree that 2008 has been a remarkable year for the NHS. It has marked the 60th anniversary celebrations of the establishment of the Health Service with notable landmark achievements of which all those who have worked, contributed and helped to develop this national institution and treasure should be proud. On the financial front, it has been the year in which colleagues across the country have been working to reposition the NHS to secure financial stability in order to deliver effective organisational performance. But 2008 has also afforded us the time to look ahead and the publication of the Lord Darzi Review offers much scope for us to work at all levels towards a more patient responsive service.

Here in the NHS North West, 2008 has also been significant on several fronts. We have achieved some notable performance results and ratings as attested by the Healthcare Commission Annual Health Check and you will agree that these results are due to the leadership and contributions that our people have made. The success of our organisations at providing excellence and world class standards is also dependent on the continuing development of our leaders and of their contributions at creating effective leadership 'top down' and 'front line up' to engage, involve and support all of our people to deliver of their best.

It is also timely that 2008 also marks the first anniversary of the NHS NW Leadership Academy, the vehicle for creating a platform for excellence in leadership and strategy development through nurturing, supporting and sustaining talent and leadership development across the North West. The Academy has within one year developed a robust and innovative set of strategies for:

- Building on, and delivering on the National Talent Management and Leadership approach

- Identification of individual potential
- Developing and supporting that potential
- Tracking individual talent
- Ensuring a sustainable pipeline of future leaders.

Through a systematic programme of seminars, workshops, masterclasses, executive immersion, stretch programmes and study tours, the NW has been able to create and strengthen a community of practice for leadership development. Of equal importance is the Academy's commitment to knowledge transfer and sharing of good practice through a variety of vehicles such as newsletters, thought leadership postcards, toolkits and this publication, *Placing Ladders: harnessing our leadership potential.* It brings together a set of thought pieces and stories of personal experiences, learning and leadership practices by leaders to engage hearts and minds of our people. The stories are wide ranging and personal, but they convey insights and reflections that can help us all to have conversations about the futures we want to co-create to harness the efforts of all our people to deliver excellence in the care and services we provide.

Mike Farrar, CBE
Chief Executive, NHS NW

INTRODUCTION

Julian Hartley

I am delighted to introduce *Placing Ladders: harnessing our leadership potential* which brings together a range of leadership stories from the NHS North West Chief Executive community. The book offers the chance for us to share our leadership experiences – good and bad – and reflect on the challenges we have faced and how these have been overcome.

Good leadership in the NHS is a central theme of the Next Steps Review and here in the North West we have already established a strong leadership community among Chief Executives and other senior NHS leaders through support from the NHS North West Leadership Academy as a membership organisation. The Academy has responded to the priorities of its members by commissioning a wide range of leadership development programmes. In addition, the Academy has a commitment to sharing the abundance of good leadership practice across the North West as well as bringing in expertise from national and international figures.

It is in the spirit of sharing leadership stories and experiences that this book is published. The stories are wide ranging and reflect different approaches by the contributors, but all are united by the goal of leading teams, organisations and systems to benefit the patients we serve. I want to thank all of those who have offered to contribute and to invite further leadership stories from colleagues who are moved to offer them after reading this book.

1

ON PLACING LADDERS

Deborah Chafer

I n our brochure promoting the launch of the NHS North West Leadership Academy, the work of Stephen Covey (1989) was cited as follows:

> 'Management is the efficiency of climbing the ladder of success: Leadership determines whether the ladder is leaning against the right wall.'

Covey's ideas, like that of other thought leaders, usually generate a lot of food for thought. In a few lines here we are offered two views which trigger off a set of further thoughts about what is distinctive about management and what is distinctive about leadership. The metaphor of the ladder will evoke a range of images, ideas and thoughts, and colleagues who have seen Covey's quote above may derive a variety of insights and reach varying conclusions, but here is one example of this which was also quoted in the brochure as follows:

> 'Today's NHS Leaders don't face their multiple challenges alone: our leaders have teams, directorates or organisations to meet the challenges and achieve goals. Our job as leaders is not to come up with solutions alone, but to inspire the people we lead to place ladders together, against the most appropriate walls.'

> Mike Farrar: Chief Executive, NHS North West

Emphasis on challenges, yes, but strength in teams and organisations, collaborative working and inspirational leadership to achieve goals appears a fitting vision as to what we should be focusing on. And whilst there will be several interpretations on the metaphor, 'placing ladders' seems an appropriate title for our book on leadership. We see it as a means of sharing ideas about engagement, inspiring the people we work with to deliver on the challenges set out in the most recent of NHS agendas.

It is also opportune for thinking afresh about engaging and inspiring our people in view of the need for service transformation which has been given added impetus by the recently published Lord Darzi Report, *Healthier Horizons in the North West.*

The Next Stage Review with its emphasis on a 'service that empowers staff and gives patients choice' provides a great opportunity for working, learning, sharing and finding new ways of leading and engaging. Perhaps most importantly of all is that it offers us a chance to have meaningful conversations at all levels of our organisations as to how we can most effectively respond and engage, all our people, in delivering quality care.

It is known, but should be reinforced through conversations, that delivering service improvement is everybody's business. It is vital and necessary that leaders at all levels of our organisations, from executive/board level through to departmental/unit, and crucially front line leaders, engage and harness the 'collective imagination of [our] people, encouraging and enabling them to join the transformation journey... to motivate [our] staff to full commitment and spur them on to make that extra effort' (Kets de Vries, 2005).

There is convincing evidence in the management literature from across sectors which points to the need for leaders at all levels to '*understand the way people in their organisations behave* ... to *create and sustain relationships to deliver on service improvement*' and to adapt their own behaviour to '*lead in a creative and motivating way*' (Kets de Vries, 2005)

So what are the head line issues on placing ladders against appropriate walls for us all? They must include:

- Setting direction and articulating vision
- Creating context and opportunity
- Inspiring, encouraging, enabling and motivating others
- Creating, nurturing and sustaining relationships.

These are all important. Leadership affects us all; we not only experience the impact of others leadership but we also exercise it. This point was well made in a short article by Bell (2007) who is also expanding his ideas further in this book of readings when he suggested that:

'Leadership is all about providing focus and relevance to the activities people are engaged in, and enabling them to be "the best they can be", whatever part they play ... leaders and leadership are needed at all levels of the system.'

In our aspiration to provide world class health care, we recognise the need for world class leaders. Our NHS community is made up of very able and inspiring leaders and we believe that there is much value in sharing thoughts, ideas and helping to make explicit the role that we can all contribute to delivering quality care.

Placing Ladders is a book of stories by some of our CEOs in the North West. Our starting point was based on the realisation that stories on leadership and management are powerful rhetorical devices for engaging hearts and minds. In terms of impact and popularity, books on management and leadership that are based on storytelling, personal stories or case studies, metaphors, allegories, parables and reflective accounts win hands down: Blanchard & Bowles' (1998) allegory on people engagement entitled *Gung Ho*, Spencer Johnson's (1992) book on change management, *Who Moved My Cheese?*, Stephen Lundin's (2000) focus on staff morale, *Fish*, or for that matter Eliyahu Goldratt & Jeff Cox's (2002) *The Goal*, are cases in point and have sold millions.

A key feature of these accounts relates to the manner of the storytelling or storyteller and the way in which they engage our feelings and emotions and the actions or behaviours that they evoke in us. Although at face value, they lack the theoretical underpinning associated with academic texts and publications, it can be argued that they are designed to appeal more to our 'touchy-feely' and emotional selves. They also have a compelling effect in causing us to think new thoughts and about our own roles and behaviours.

The power of these accounts resides in the way in which the storytelling, the language and the ideas are woven together to convey insightful and at times significant insights. They also stimulate conversations and enable us to make sense and co-create actions for improvement for ourselves and patient care. Additionally, we feel that *Placing Ladders* is about conveying the stories from leaders to leaders to trigger off conversations about who we are and what we do, how we can work and learn more effectively, and how we can support each other at giving of our best to those we serve.

Stories can be inspirational, but they should set us to think and act in different ways and to do what we will need to reflect and study the ideas and messages behind them. We have anchored our starting point to the work of Covey. Many of us would have bought and read his *The 7 Habits of Highly Effective People.*

Dan Bobinski (2008), the training specialist and author, cited a story by a colleague of his at a workshop in which the trainer asked, 'How many people here have read *7 Habits?*' Over half of the 100 or so delegates stood up. He then asked them to stay standing if they can remember three of the seven habits. More than half of those standing sat down. He then asked those standing to stay standing if they can recite all seven habits. Only three people remained standing. Finally, he said, 'If you are living all seven habits in your life, remain standing.' The remaining three people sat down.

In case this little story has caused you to think about Covey's *7 Habits*, here's a chance for you to reflect on the same by inserting what you can recall of the habits proposed by Covey:

Habit 1:

Habit 2:

Habit 3:

Habit 4:

Habit 5:

Habit 6:

Habit 7:

Stories, and books on stories of leadership for that matter, are useful but they require us to do something more that just reading them. We hope that the stories by our leaders will be read, digested and used in conversations so that insights and ideas derived from them can be learnt and practised in everyday work. Moreover, we hope that you will also see the stories come alive in the actions and behaviours of the leaders themselves and others through effective role modelling.

And as we are talking about matters Seven, Carmine Gallo's (2007) book, *Fire Them Up*, explores the importance of inspiration, i.e. seven simple secrets for inspiring others that we can all practise and role model as follows:

SECRET 1: **Ignite your enthusiasm** – light a fire in your own heart before you start theirs as inspiration really begins with us.

SECRET 2: **Navigate the way** and offer a specific, consistent and memorable vision as simple and clear messages win hearts.

SECRET 3: **Sell the benefit** – speak with commitment.

SECRET 4: **Paint a picture – tell powerful, memorable and actionable stories** – as Howard Gardner (2006) has observed … 'stories speak to both parts of the human mind – its reason and emotion.'

SECRET 5: **Invite participation** – listen to and invite participation

SECRET 6: **Reinforce an optimistic outlook** – remember the link between optimism and inspiration is direct and immediate.

SECRET 7: **Encourage their potential** – 'People connect with people, not things. And the best compliment you can receive from another human being is this: 'You make me want to be a better person.' … Motivation is about bringing out the best in people, but people will not listen to your message until they know you care.

In essence, the stories in this book are our stories and their sole purpose is to share and communicate leadership aspirations. They include thought pieces, stories, reflections, learning derived from inspirational writers, leaders, figures, works etc. that have made an impact on the 'softer skills' on the lives and character of our leaders which can 'bring confidence to our organisations and ensures that good ideas are surfaced, celebrated and acted upon'. We believe that such a collection could serve a major role on impacting on the collective leadership effort of all our people.

At the outset though, there are a number of influences that have shaped our approach. In this outline introductory chapter we would like to make contact with some of these ideas. The next 15 chapters will provide detail accounts of the stories.

In 1979, a study entitled *Management and Communication in the Office of the Future* was submitted as a PhD thesis in the Department of Philosophy, University of California at Berkeley. The study was carried out by Fernando Flores whose name is not usually associated as a major figure in leadership circles, but in many ways has made a major contribution in more ways than one.

Flores is an interesting figure. Tags of engineer, philosopher, business consultant, entrepreneur, businessman, as well as politician, are usually attached to his name. In 1970, at the age of 28, he became finance minister in the government of Salvador Allende in Chile. But the 1970s were testing times in Chile [and elsewhere] in South America and the political strife that led to the death of Allende also resulted in a 3-year spell of imprisonment for Flores. Although enduring a very difficult time whilst in prison, Flores was able to make time contemplating the role of computers for communication rather than for computation.

In 1976, Flores won his release through the efforts of Amnesty International and others and emigrated to the States with his wife and five children. Once there he promptly enrolled for doctoral studies at Stanford, partially with support from his wife working as a sandwich wrapper, and his teenage children with their Burger King wages. Flores study focused initially on fundamental questions relating to what it means to be human. He drew heavily from the work of the German philosopher Martin Heidegger, from whom he learnt that 'existence arises from interaction' and of the value and importance of 'speech acts', i.e. how words [language] we use in our everyday interaction 'always conveys not merely information but commitment'.

Flores went on to become a very successful businessman, educator and consultant and his ideas, extensive writings, and some would say his way of being, still has a lasting impact. Flores argues that:

> 'Human society operates through the expression of requests and promises ... a business, likewise, is a collection of simultaneous conversations and every conversation involves an act of commitment ... in this network of commitments, everyone is a customer, a provider, or both at once.'

He argued that our identities, be they personal or organisational, should be grounded in our personal style and in our commitments – what some refer to as being authentic.

Flores believes that 'commitment is what creates real change' and that mastering 'speech acts', i.e. using language rituals that build trust between colleagues and customers, enables people to see new possibilities. Speech acts are powerful because most of the actions that people engage in, whether in business or their personal lives, are carried out through conversation. Flores' studies have led him to conclude that 'most people speak without intention; they simply say whatever comes to mind. Speak with intention, and your actions take on new purpose.' Speak with commitment or with passion, speak with concern or with warmth and you act with commitment, passion, concern or warmth.

Harriet Rubin's (1998) short pieces about Flores suggest that there is 'magic in Fernando Flores: the magic of transformation. Like any true magician who transforms things – or, in this case, people – Flores is not content to describe the act of transformation ... he performs it.'

Flores' view as to how our thinking affects our behaviour can be summed up as operating at three levels [or realms]. The first, and the most self-limiting, is that of *What You Know You Know*. This is a self-contained world, in which people are unwilling to risk their identity in order to take on new challenges. The second and richer realm is *What You Don't Know*. This is the realm that causes anxiety or boredom. These are things about life, our family, our work, that we do not know about. A natural coping mechanism for most of us is to blur *What You Don't Know* with *What You Know You Know*. But Flores believes that we should all aspire to the level of the third realm i.e. *What You Don't Know You Don't Know*. It is here that we can see opportunities that we're normally too blind to see. It is here that we see without bias: Flores proposes that the language of this realm is the language of truth, which requires trust.

For Flores then, **communication with commitment, truth, and trust are at the heart of power** and this is the key message that we want to share and instil across our communities. The starting point though is our ourselves. Leadership is about us as individuals, the way we communicate, our commitment and passion, the level of trust we exhibit and our credibility amongst other factors.

Several other commentators have identified the key qualities that leaders need to demonstrate in a transformational context. Of these qualities we believe that one in particular, i.e. 'foresight', can impact on service transformation in a major way and in this regard we want to draw on the work and ideas of Joseph Jaworski:

> 'Few would argue that foresight is central to the task of exercising leadership. It is the mark of a leader, taking initiative, going out ahead to show the way. It's what gives the leader his or her "lead". Can foresight be reliably developed in rising leaders and in collectives of those charged with leadership? If so, by what process?
>
> This domain – the deeper dimensions of enhanced decision making, the capacity to sense and actualise emerging futures – lies largely unexplored in current management research and in our understanding of leadership in general. It is a domain that is both deeply personal and inherently systemic. It requires examining who we are and the source from which we operate, both individually and collectively.'

So says Joseph Jaworski (1996), the author of *Synchronicity: The Inner Path of Leadership* (Berrett-Koehler Publishers). Joseph's story as a thought leader began after he turned his back on a successful law career. A series of connections with remarkable people, including David Bohm, one of the principal architects of quantum theory, influenced his thinking.

So what does Jaworski think about leadership?

> 'Most leadership programs begin with a description of the attributes of the leader – a leader has vision, a leader has courage, a leader inspires others. All of that's fine; it's very important. But what's leadership really

all about? To me, leadership is a journey towards wholeness. A leader's journey starts by looking inward to understand: Why am I here? What is it that I'm here to do?'

Jaworski's view of leadership is simple: ... before you can lead others, before you can help others, you have to discover yourself. Today a leader can't impose himself/herself on others. He/she needs to make themselves available to others. And nothing is more powerful than someone who knows who they are ... if you know what you're all about and where you're heading, you become more AUTHENTIC ... and if you know who you are, you become more CREDIBLE and people trust you.

There is considerable pressure on organisations to deliver results and quality. Many also understand that the things they have tried don't go far enough. Jaworski believes that:

> '... the top leadership team in an organisation has to commit itself to a journey of self-discovery. And the leaders have to provide space for other people in the organisation to do the same. If you want a creative explosion to take place, if you want the kind of performance that leads to truly exceptional results, you have to be willing to embark on a journey that leads to an alignment between an individual's personal values and aspirations and the organisation's values and aspirations.'

The key messages from Joseph Jaworksi can be summed up as follows:

- Leadership at all levels will be necessary in order to show how transformation can be fostered by attitudes of genuine openness and curiosity, supporting reflection and inquiry and tapping into the deepest sources of individual and collective aspiration;
- Leadership at all levels will be effective through personal and team learning;
- Leaders at all levels will need to understand how their own personal journey is inextricably linked to their organisation's future;
- Leaders at all levels will need to engage in learning through the use of foresight as a basis for deeper dimensions of transformational leadership.

The challenges facing leaders can be onerous. But with foresight, leaders can create leaders who can engage people through communication with commitment, truth and trust. From Gandhi to Mandela, the mantra is the same. We should be the change we want to see and the starting point is ourselves. Placing ladders provide us with a starting point to say who we are, what we believe in and how we can make a difference by working, learning and leading together. Above all it is a starting point for us to have conversations about the futures we want to co-create and how we can harness our collective strength to make this happen.

And just in case you are still thinking about Covey's 7 habits, here they are:

1. **Be proactive.**
2. **Begin with the end in mind.**
3. **Put first things first.**
4. **Think win-win.**
5. **Seek first to understand, then to be understood.**
6. **Synergise.**
7. **Sharpen the saw.**

Don't be too busy to stop and sharpen your saw ... then commit:

'Until one is committed, there is hesitancy, the chance to draw back, always ineffectiveness. Concerning all acts of initiative and creation, there is one elementary truth the ignorance of which kills countless ideas and splendid plans: that the moment one definitely commits oneself, then providence moves too. All sorts of things occur to help one that would never otherwise have occurred. A whole stream of events arise from the decision, raising in one's favour all manner of unforeseen incidents, meetings and material assistance which no man could have dreamed would have come his way. Whatever you can do or dream you can, begin it. Boldness has genius, power and magic in it. Begin it now.'

Goethe, Johann Wolfgang Von

References

Bell, A. (2007) Leading from the front. The Health Foundation. http://www.health.org.uk/news/features/leadership_1.html.

Blanchard, K. & Bowles, S. (1998) *Gung Ho*. London: Harper Collins.

Bobinski, D. (2008) Read any good books lately? So What? http://www.management-issues.com/2008/9/25/opinion/read-any-good-books-lately-so-what.asp.

Covey, S. (1989) *The Seven Habits of Highly Effective People*. New York: Fireside.

Flores, F. (1979) Management and Communication in the Office of the Future. Doctoral Thesis submitted to University of California, Berkeley.

Gallo, C. (2007) *Fire Them Up*. New Jersey: Wiley.

Gardner, H. (2006) *Five Minds for the Future*. Boston: Harvard Business School Press.

Goldratt, E. & Cox, J. (2002) *The Goal: A Process of Ongoing Improvement*. Hampshire, UK: Gower.

Jaworski, J. (1996) *Synchronicity: The Inner Path of Leadership*. San Francisco: Berrett-Koehler.

Johnson, S. (1992) *Who Moved My Cheese?* New York: G.P. Putnams.

Kets de Vries, M. (2005) *The Global Executive Leadership Inventory*. San Francisco: Pfeiffer/Wiley.

Lundin, S. (2000) *A Remarkable Way to Boost Morale and Improve Results*. New York: Hyperion.

Rubin, H. (1998) The power of words. http://www.fastcompany.com/magazine/21/flores.html?page=0%2C5.

2

LEADERSHIP FOR IMPROVEMENT:
WINNING HEARTS MORE THAN MINDS

Anthony Bell

I can't honestly claim to have been inspired to work in the NHS from a young age, although without doubt the fact that both my parents were nurses influenced the environment in which I grew up, as is the case with so many children. As an adolescent, I had already made the bold and non-conformist decision as is typical of youth, to be something different to my parents when I left school.

So I left school at 16 years and went off to be an apprentice fitter and all was fine until I ended up in hospital as a consequence of a bad renal infection. It was there that I first began to understand what it was that nurses did and how their patients valued them. It was more of a dawning realisation than a sudden revelation that I came to understand just how much of a difference one could make to people's lives. The combination of skill, knowledge, humour and humanity had made its impact not only on the care I was fortunate enough to receive, but in what I witnessed during that short time as a patient. More than anything, I suppose it was the appeal of the responsibility and the ability to 'do good' that made its indelible mark on my subconscious.

I entered nurse training at the age of 18 years having sat the GNC entrance exam and having done just well enough to train to be a Registered Nurse. I trained in a district general hospital and was all too well aware that most male counterparts were only entered for enrolled nurse training at the time. So from an early stage in my career, I was acutely aware of the need to prove myself and aim for better than average in my various exams and assessments. I learnt a lot about the gender divide in those early days and its influence in the workplace. I found myself in a female-dominated profession where the male minority was tolerated but not always welcome and indeed, viewed with some suspicion by both colleagues and patients – until that is, they got the chance to know you.

I specialised in Accident & Emergency and Trauma Nursing for most of my clinical career and worked in different hospitals undertaking specialist training and doing the things you do to progress your understanding, skill level and ability to undertake a variety of roles. In all of that time and what was to follow, I have come to realise just how important some people were to my progression. I had observed and been influenced by people in leadership roles from an early stage. Some of them were awe-inspiring in terms of their ability to manage crises, motivate teams and deal with triumph and disaster in equal measure.

I had also experienced the opposite and its effect not just on me but on patients and their families. Perhaps it was this stark contrast and its impact for better or worse that stimulated something in me to say – 'I want to be that awe-inspiring leader who makes a positive difference' (not much challenge there then!). When you know things can be better than what you see in front of you and you've had experience of what 'better' looks like, you're well on the way to starting your own journey just as they had done.

It was this that made me realise I wanted to be like that A&E Sister who everyone trusted to get it right every time – like my Clinical Tutor in A&E who inspired me to become a Clinical Tutor; like the Nursing Officer that showed me there was more to getting things right than having specialty-based knowledge; and like the Director of Nursing who so expertly influenced the non-nursing community of the Hospital to listen to what nurses had to say and got nurses to open their eyes to the roles and responsibilities of the wider team. In all of these and many more role models, I had encountered people who cared about what they did, how they did it and took an interest in me following in their footsteps.

I came to realise that these traits were not simply the province of nurses; they existed in every walk of health care and that what singled them out was their ability to lead from the front. These Consultants, Nurses, Estates Managers, Therapists, Chairmen, Chief Executives weren't in it for the status; they achieved the status through recognition of what they did and how they did it – they went the extra mile and 'Walked the Talk'.

They made a visible difference. They demanded a lot of themselves and a lot of the people who worked with them and in return, gave much back in terms of their commitment to developing colleagues who shared their passion and energy to push boundaries and be better than 'good enough'. I was lucky enough during a point in my career to attend an Assessment Centre for aspiring leaders in Nursing. I learnt not only my own development needs and strengths, but more importantly, the degree to which I could influence others if I could master some of the complex skills that go with managing people and reconciling what might appear at times to be impossible demands.

At one point in my career I decided to cross the divide and became a Director of Joint Commissioning with a Health Authority. The fact that I had no experience in this area at all before entering it did not daunt me, such was my super-confidence and naivety. I did know however that I was capable of learning and, of course, I understood what needed to be commissioned because I had absolute clarity from a service provider point of view. Needless to say, it was a steep learning curve.

What struck me most about this experience was the overwhelming need that confronted people and systems and its seductive simplicity. Meeting that need in a meaningful way to patients, families and carers was a far harder task than some things I had come across in the acute hospital setting.

I realised that for things to improve, the system needed to change – a relatively simple procedure of getting an elderly patient out of a hospital bed who no longer needed or wished to be there demanded leadership, innovation and flexibility at all levels. Intermediate care was a concept, not a reality, and so it had to be developed. Doctors and nurses needed to develop knowledge and skills on the appropriate usage of resources and patients had to have confidence in the standards of care. Social Services needed assurance about the integrity of assessment and funding mechanisms.

Finally, as with all things, none of this would have been developed until we committed to action and started to 'just do it'. We converted a community hospital into our first Intermediate Care Unit and started the whole process. We had to deal with political and public opposition to what was seen as a hospital closure and had to sell the benefits of the new system. Most of all at commissioner, doctor, nurse, social worker level – we had to deliver. What was also obvious was that simply pouring more money into the same system that was already failing was not the answer. To paraphrase Peter Senge and Don Berwick [amongst others], if we did what we had always done then we would simply get what we had always got! We now have a number of such facilities in the system and Intermediate care has developed much further.

We all know that the NHS is characterised by its complexity and reliance on large numbers of people working in large, medium- and small-sized organisations. From Strategic Health Authorities, Primary Care Trusts, Foundation Hospitals, Acute and Community Trusts, to GP Practices, all are engaged and working to achieve aims that span from an individual patient to a whole population.

And as we all know, in any business activity, it is the complexity of the task and its dependence on people interacting that requires visible leadership. Leadership is all about providing focus and relevance to the activities people are engaged in, and enabling them to be 'the best they can be', whatever part they play.

Therefore, leaders and leadership are needed at all levels of the system. The person providing direction, context, support and inspiration may be the Chief Executive, but is equally likely to be the Ward Sister, Consultant, Porter or Therapist. It's not the title that defines the leader but what they do and what they make possible for others to achieve.

Leaders help people and the teams within which they work to re-frame their thinking and get beyond the rhetoric of the moment to what really matters. All too often, targets are cited as the problem. Whether reducing hospital acquired infection, waiting times, lengths of stay or food wastage, the leader is the person who helps others see the advantage to patients and sets about taking action to achieve the goal. They build an irresistible force for change that others want to follow.

Leaders emerge in organisations in a variety of situations and it's the job of managers to create an environment in which their skills and motivation can be guided, encouraged, supported and recognised. Improving service quality and the patient experience needs to be seen as the responsibility of the whole organisation and the impact should resonate right through to the bottom line of the balance sheet.

Efficiency drive

Doing things inefficiently robs health care organisations and patients of new opportunities for future service developments and threatens the very existence of those that we provide today. It's the job of leaders to articulate this in a way that staff can relate to. The whole organisation needs to understand the benefits of a philosophy of continuous improvement and its ability to realise real benefits for patients. Realising these benefits requires us all to commit to continuous learning and doing that can result in effective practice and service improvement.

The move toward greater efficiency is a global requirement of all health care providers. In some cases there will be big numbers produced through better procurement programmes etc. In many cases, however, the savings will be more modest and focused on improving care. For instance, in taking Lean thinking methodology forward across the Trust, we have incorporated our PCT partners to ensure 'end-to-end' solutions that improve outcomes, patient experience and reduce duplication costs.

Little things about who does what, where and when in a process can greatly improve the patient's experience and reduce transaction costs. Shifting more pre-op screening into the community; transferring our outpatient dispensing to a local retail pharmacy by means of a joint venture; reducing new patient to follow up ratios; managing patients with acute cellulitis at home with IV antibiotics through the community nursing service; managing DVT patients at home with daily thrombolytic injections are all examples of process improvement that has reduced the need for costly hospitalisation and improved the experience for the patient.

More recently, we opened a cohort ward for patients with *C. Diff*. By bringing such patients together and focusing care standards for this type of infection in one area, we saw a dramatic reduction in the number of reported cases whilst throughput in other wards increased as their side room facilities became free of patients that would otherwise have blocked the room for days and require considerable nursing resource. The reduction in numbers of cases has of course been felt in staffing budgets and drug costs reductions, let alone the obvious benefit to patients who might otherwise have contracted such an infection. The point is that these initiatives have been clinically developed, managerially supported and driven by leaders from various backgrounds.

Whenever organisations embark on anything that involves change, there will be a high degree of anxiety and sometimes cynicism among staff. Preparation is essential and sticking with it when the going gets tough is fundamental. It's like the practice of 'good medicine' – a lot of art and a bit of science.

The art and science come together at the outset by taking some simple baseline measures of where you are in terms of service delivery and making it clear where you want to be. Clear communication at all levels from leaders is critical. Staff need to understand the big picture just as much as those at the Board level. Indeed, they need to own the vision and accept at times that their efforts may be realised in benefits elsewhere in the organisation.

Making a £50,000 saving in food wastage in a year may not result in more money being pumped into the catering budget but may pay for a nurse specialist or avoid the redundancy of another key member of staff. Either of these results would be beneficial to patients.

Similarly, avoiding or reducing prescribing costs, seeing a higher ratio of new patients to follow-up patients in clinics or simply putting the right type of non-clinical waste in the right coloured bag can have dramatic effects and similar benefits. Behavioural change needs to take place at both the individual and organisational level. A 1% improvement from 3,000 staff is worth more than a 20% improvement from 30 staff. Our role as leaders at all levels is to sustain engagement, widen involvement and increase aspirations beyond the 1%.

What can we learn from best in class companies

Whether in the public or private sector, the 'best in class' organisations have a core set of values in common. They pursue customer focus and cost reduction relentlessly to maintain their position as world-class leaders. They focus more on engaging with their staff and learning together than they do on analysing the detail of budgets to the point of endless debate and inaction.

Organisations can't innovate and stay ahead if they are constantly in a state of retrospective analysis. They get the information they need to a level of 'good enough' and then commit to change. They anticipate the need for review and correction along the way to keep them on course.

In any year of a five-year programme of improvement, our organisation will have built in 90-day targets and reviews. Finally, we ensure that we communicate the successes and patient benefits to all staff through face-to-face briefings from Board. In the midst of continuous change, staff need to know how they are doing, and nothing works better than the recognition of success.

Communicating with the organisation is essential and the more means and methods available, the better. Getting staff involved at the outset is important and Open Space events have been a useful precursor for me in securing engagement and ownership. It's important to have a clear idea of what the issues are and what the change is that you see is needed and to communicate this. Equally it's vital to get staff connected not just to the logic of the case for change but, more importantly, the emotional attachment with it. Open Space, and its capacity to help us to create the vision and ways and means of change, offer us considerable opportunities for meaningful conversations, both within and beyond our organisations.

It is this attachment, in my experience that will drive the behavioural change required to deliver real impact and improvement. It is through this winning of hearts more than minds that values get put into action. Jack Welch, CEO of GE, once said that he never claimed to be a great manager or visionary leader but as an Irishman – he knew how to tell a good story! We all need to share our story; that is our personal call for transformational change. Using processes like Open Space events, staff briefings, blogs, newsletters, improvement events etc., are a way of making it personal. When people can see the Board is committed, and in particular the CEO, it gives them permission to get committed too and when they do that, they begin to own the story for themselves and make it personal and relevant to their own people.

In conclusion I feel that, whilst we must continue to make exhortations for higher aspirations, we should also value and, yes celebrate, the contributions and efforts of our people. There is a lot of very good practice out there. There is also a lot of useful literature from both sides of the Atlantic to give us the evidence to support our work on service improvement: Bibby & Reinertsen (2004) briefing on *Leading for Improvement; whose job is it any way;* Reinertsen's (2004) *A Theory of Leadership for the Transformation for Healthcare Organisations* and Ovretveit's (2004) review of *The Leader's role in Quality and Safety Improvement* are cases in point.

Equally important are the plethora of useful resources emanating from the NHS Institute of Improvement and Innovation as well as the Institute of Healthcare Improvement [IHI] and others. As James Reinertsen reminds us, the challenge is for us to have ongoing conversations and action to:

- Keep reframing our core cultural values;
- Creating and sustaining our improvement capability;
- Collaborating across our competitive boundaries;
- Creating an environment that can impact on business performance [results] and organisational/community benefit;
- Improve at system rather than at project level only; and
- Maintain constancy of purpose over the long-term transformational journey.

References

Bibby, J. & Reinertsen, J.L. (2004) *Leading for Improvement: Whose Job is it Anyway?* NHS Modernisation Agency.

Reinertsen, J.L. (2004) A theory of leadership for the transformation for health care organisations. IHI White Paper

Ovretveit, J. (2004) *The Leader's Role in Quality and Safety Improvement.* Stockholm: ACC.

3

MAKING SPACES

Phil Morley

December 2005

Mrs Brookes sat at the very front of her chair. Stiff, self contained with a closed-up face, her hands tightly clenched, her eyes cold and empty, bleak like a winter's morning. I had been at the Trust just over four weeks as Director of Turnaround – there was so much to do. Mrs Brookes was angry. Mrs Brookes was lost. Mrs Brookes was alone.

Slowly, without bitterness, yet with infinite regret, she told me her story. A month ago she was rushed into hospital with her husband. He had suffered a large heart attack. They had been married for three months shy of 50 years. He was very poorly. She was desperately worried. 'I didn't want to leave him you know. They made me go home,' she said. The story went on … it was the first night of their married life they had been apart. 'I asked the nurse four times to call me if anything happened. She promised me – she promised me.' It was a busy shift; you know how manic the winter is. The ward was short-staffed. Mr Brookes worsened. Three times he asked for his wife, three times he assumed she was on her way. No one phoned. Mrs Brookes sat up all night – watching the phone. It was silent. Wearily she made her way to the hospital the next morning, half in hope, half in dark despair, but she kept telling herself they haven't called; he must be getting better. She walked onto the ward. Staff were too busy to stop and talk. She walked to his bedside. Someone else was in his place. Panic welled up inside her. 'Where's Alfred?' she shouted. The patient in the next bed had the answer. 'Sorry love,' he said. 'Your husband died in the night. He was asking for you at the end you know …'

Slowly the tears trickled down Mrs Brookes' face as she finished her story. 'He shouldn't have died alone. I never got the chance to say goodbye.'

She looked up; her piercing grey eyes met mine. The stiffness returned to her body, steel in her voice. 'All I want is for the nurse who was in charge to say sorry. Is that too much to ask?'

Apparently it was. The nurse refused to meet Mrs Brookes. It was management's fault. If we'd had more staff; if there were more beds; if morale wasn't so low. Her trade union said we couldn't force her to meet 'the relative', the RCN agreed. So Mrs Brookes came to me. I sat watching her quiet dignity, a frail broken old lady who just wanted someone to say sorry.

Making spaces

Ever wondered what it is that makes a ladder work 'work'. A simple design, a framework and hey presto – potential, functionality, reach and, above all, possibility. Yet stop a moment and think … As you pause to view the framework of the ladder, have you ever considered that it is the spaces in between the rungs that truly create the possibilities? If all the rungs were together it would be completely useless. At the same time, if the rungs were too far apart (the spaces are too big) then all you have is potential that is achingly out of reach. You have holes!

If we are using ladders as the metaphor for changing organisations or changing culture, values, belief systems, whatever – then it is the spaces in between where we should focus our efforts.

Change is a coin with two sides. One side is the improvement science. The hard, tangible, 'real' things that one can alter, adapt, re-engineer or re-design. Things like systems, processes, structures, job roles, room designs, hardware, software, reporting lines, accountabilities, etc.

Yet the other side (relational practice) is where we so often fail to consider – the side where beliefs, values, behaviours, paradigms and culture live; the soft, intangible, insubstantial, hard-to-define things. Yet we ignore these at our peril.

For change will only ever be an improvement, sustainable and renewing, if we are cognisant of both sides of the coin. For however many times a coin lands on 'heads', you know that it always going to land 'tails-up' at some point.

Many change endeavours in the NHS have been successful with the improvement science side of the coin. Look at the achievements of the Modernisation Agency, the impact of targets and standards, new roles, the development of lean healthcare, the high impact interventions – all fabulous examples of change, improvement and breakthrough developments. Yet none has been the panacea – the nirvana, the holy grail, for which we so long. I have been in the health service now for 26 years and despite the major changes in provision, in access, in waiting times, in treatment regimes, in organisational structures and hierarchies, in funding, and in management practice, we still fail the Mr & Mrs Brookes of this world time and time again.

Is it because we are fundamentally hard people or because we have lost the compulsion to care? No, I cannot believe that. Is it that the creativity and intellect is gone? Never. I work with some of the most imaginative, dynamic, inventive and innovative people I have ever known. I believe, quite simply, that as leaders in Healthcare we have spent too long on the rungs; we've forgotten to spend time creating the spaces in between.

We have majored on what is complicated rather than what is complex. Maybe now, maybe today as we embark once more on significant upheaval in the way we commission and provide Healthcare (Darzi, localism, world class commissioning, Quality focus), we can as leaders build into our organisations not only the rungs of our ladders but create the spaces in between at the same time.

Space to start

Creating spaces doesn't just happen. It is emergent, yes, but it needs careful planning, thinking and designing too. Don't be fooled; it is just as rigorous and difficult as planning the rungs. For me, there are six spaces an organisation needs to consider. Each of these is a stretch – too little and there is no movement, too much and the risk is too great and there is only failure. Creating spaces is also the work of more than one individual. The whole Executive Team and the Board need to be behind this space-making. Holding the uncertainty, living with the ambiguity, challenging the unhelpful responses, modelling the desired behaviours, taking the difficult decisions, keeping on 'keeping on' ... The best leaders have the best teams. It sounds like a simple truism but without the backing of your top team you create not spaces but holes. An old boss once told me: 'You cannot soar with eagles when you're running with turkeys.' The job of the leader is to put the team out that has the best chance of winning. Winning for the organisation, winning for the staff, winning for the patients, winning for Mr & Mrs Brookes!

It has been my privilege at Mid Cheshire to have a team that is stimulating, challenging, creative and supportive. They let me get away with nothing, yet give me everything. You owe it to yourself, the members of your team and every patient who walks through your doors to have the best team. This is the first space – the space to start. It doesn't mean you need a team of experts, nor experienced old hands who have been around the block a few times. Nor does it mean a team of intellects with the brain size of planets. It does mean a team of energy, enthusiasm, commitment to the best possible outcomes for patients. A team that is willing to bleed for the organisation; a team who is strong enough to challenge you as a leader; a team that draws its strength from being vulnerable with each other. You have no space for passengers. No time for nay-sayers (those who say 'yes' when together and say 'no' behind closed doors) and you have to realise that sometimes each of them may need to drive the bus! I have discovered as Chief Executive that the Persians had a great truth. In the Persian court it was hard to tell the Emperor anything other than what he wanted to hear. He had the power of life and death over every subject. How then would he ever know what was 'real'? In the Court, each Emperor had a 'truth-teller'. The one person who (in private) would swear, when asked, to tell the Emperor the truth. The Emperor's commitment, when appointing his truth-teller, was not to behead the poor fellow if the truth was unpalatable.

Every CEO needs their truth-teller. Who is the confidante? Who is the one person you can be vulnerable with, who can whisper the truth that others fear to speak? I urge everyone in positions of great responsibility to find your truth-teller and let them know what it is you expect from them and honour that relationship. The space to start is with you as leader. You set the tone; you set the language for the organisation; you give permissions for behaviours; you are the role model. You have to be both the heart and the backbone for the organisation. Every word, every action, every decision is noted and remembered. You are always on display, always being weighed in the balances, always being judged. ... You have to choose your attitude, select your interventions with care, be deliberate and discerning in your decisions.

In making space to start, I have narrowed the role of the leader down to two important areas: sense maker and storyteller. It is your job to help the organisation make sense, collectively, of the external world, of the challenges, of policies, pressures and politics, of the journey that lies ahead – the dangers to avoid, the prizes to be won. It is also your job to give direction, strategy, advice, interpretation and surety.

Whilst doing this you need to be the great storyteller. Words are power; words inspire; words create a vision metaphor, a safe place. Words are what separate man from animal. They are what created civilisation. Myths, legends and stories are what bind us together – or divide us. The leader tells their own story, weaves their own tapestry into the organisational memory. You must find your own narrative of what you stand for, of your own inspiration, and keep telling it by your words, your actions, your silences, finding new and novel ways to say the same thing over and over. Keep the story alive and evolving; pass it on so that others can tell the story, so that newcomers hear it too. Let the story breathe life and purpose into the organisation. You are the story. ... This is beginning to make the space to start.

Space to dream

'I have a dream.' We are all familiar with the words of Martin Luther King. Had he been a Chief Executive he might have said 'I have a plan' at which point everyone would have left and the world would be a different place. Dreams ignite the possibility of what might be. They cut to the heart of what keeps people going through the darkest days. Dreams warm us in our unconscious thinking; they determine our choices and often our destinies! The poetic principle says that 'not everything that can be written has yet been written'. The best leaders give individuals and the collective organisation space to dream. We might be more comfortable, in our organised scientific world, to call this visioning, but I love the thought of dream.

I recently took my organisational vision for the next five years to the Medical Advisory Committee to be ritually mauled by the Consultant Body. It was not their expected fare. At the end, one senior consultant remarked: 'It's nice to have a dream once more.' This is being the beating heart of the organisation – seeing the potential, hearing the thoughts, feeling the stirring of passions. But it cannot be just one person's dream. Movement comes when individuals can translate the dream into their own and personalise it; when it can be translated into their world and make sense for them; when the dream informs their actions and their decisions. This doesn't happen by some magical osmosis or secret incantation.

We started with a few mad ramblings of my own. My Execs were gracious enough to listen and beat this liquid ore into a more rigid shape that made sense.

When a white hot liquid is exposed to cooling it hardens. So too ideas and dreams need exposure to cold reality and careful thinking before they become firmer and more tangible. Once the metal is cool, it is still malleable. The Blacksmith then beats the metal into shape with hard blows. The role of the Board was to take the visions and dreams created and turn them into a strategy that made sense for the organisation.

But it doesn't stop there. I had the great pleasure recently of watching a master glass blower create a magnificent sculpture from a white hot glowing blob of liquid glass. Gradually a shape began to emerge; with deft application of some intricate tools, an eagle came to life. At points I thought he had finished. Under his artisan's eye the glass had taken shape and form, but was now cooling. Every so often he plunged it momentarily back into the furnace and retrieved it to add more precise shape or colour – not enough to melt the eagle away again, but enough heat to mould and shape. Gold in the same way is refined through fire. Even then, once the eagle was complete, it was far from finished. He washed and polished and filed and cleaned. It was a joy to watch.

I wonder if our dreams for our organisations are exposed to such skills, craftsmanship and honing. How does the top team allow others to add their own texture, shape and hues of colour? How can we plunge the vision back into the furnace and retain the substance but allow others to further refine it?

A dream for an organisation needs to be co-created. Maybe for some they only need to polish it so they can see it clean for themselves. For us this has meant Big Tent events, small focus groups, one-to-ones, a 'suggestives' scheme for staff, drop-in sessions, mind-mapping, workshops, a series of ward and department visits, briefing sessions. You must find ways that work for you.

As I left the glass blowing factory, I noticed a basket of cast-offs – sculptures where the glass wasn't hot enough to start or where the craftsman had let it cool too early or been too forceful with his tools. It left me wondering which of our visions have perished in the cast-off basket for want of a space to dream.

Space to appreciate

I remember quite clearly my children bringing me pictures they had drawn or cards they had made, home from school. A sense of excitement hanging over them as I walked in: 'I made this for you, Daddy!' A paper or card with a blaze of colours and shapes that may or may not be a person, mis-spelt words that sloped across the page and a look of anticipation etched on their faces as they waited for my reaction.

Did I say the obvious ... 'What on earth is this supposed to be?' Of course not. I made the appropriate oohs and aahs, exclaimed my delight and appreciation, and was rewarded with several hugs and kisses.

We are as human beings naturally appreciative, positive, supportive and encouraging. What is it about organisational constraints or constructs that beats this out of us? We take such a negative, deconstructionist, deficit-based approach to life. This isn't just healthcare; it's not just the quintessential English approach. It is an organisational paradigm that cuts deep into our psyche – a problem-solving approach, a root-cause analysis mindset. It's a 'broke, let's fix it' attitude.

When did we stop appreciating the good things that happen? When did our focus shift and all our energy go into the small number of things that go wrong? We could learn much from taking Appreciative Inquiry to the heart of our organisational constructs. This way of 'being' was first thought up by David Cooperrider, a US psychologist. It is basically a heliotropic approach; that is, things grow towards the light. Instead of holding seminars on living with darkness, leaders need to be embracing the power of shining lights into the organisation, and of watching people turning their faces towards the sun.

I'm not saying ignore what is wrong, and forget the mistakes. I am saying where is the energy of the top team? Where is the focus of the Board, and the Executives? Are you, as the leader, more curious about what goes well or what goes wrong?

At Mid Cheshire Hospitals NHS Foundation Trust, we have moved some of our Board Reports, for example, from a sickness absence target to one of attendance, from turnover to retention rates, from policies on managing sickness to improving attendance. Positive image equals positive action.

We now have annual celebration of achievement awards. Staff nominate other teams or individuals anonymously with reasons, in a number of different categories. I have been humbled by some of the comments made. One Consultant took the time to nominate nine different people with handwritten A4 pages of reasons for each individual.

We have a 'moving-on' programme for middle managers with a professional review at the end that they present to me as CEO on their development and how it impacts on their job and their team. We have anniversary lunches every quarter where staff who started in that quarter a year ago tell their story of life a year on to the Chief Executive. We have changed staff induction to 'Welcome Day'. Ward and department visits start by asking each Ward/Department Manager what are the three things they are most proud of. Executives are encouraged to write statements of support for KSF appraisals.

Each Division also runs a start-of-year event where they celebrate the achievements of last year and look ahead to the challenges of the coming year. As CEO, I hold a 'clinic' once a week where any member of staff can drop in or make an appointment for a cup of tea. Part of this half day is also for senior staff to bring with them someone they want to praise in front of me so I can share their story and say thank you too.

These are just some of the beginnings and there is always more to do, but make a start. Ensure you personally and your team and the whole organisation make space to appreciate.

Space to learn

'There should never be a learning curve when it comes to patient safety.' So read a recent report into unexpected deaths in a hospital in England. Whilst agreeing with the no-doubt honourable sentiments, it did make me smile. In healthcare the very essence of what we do is take people with no skills or training and let them practise and learn their trade – be that Doctor, Nurse, Allied Health Professional, Administrative support or even Chief Executive.

Learning is painful – it expects to make mistakes; it is iterative; sometimes costly. It takes practice, patience and perseverance. How important, how absolutely essential, is the role of leader in making space for individuals, teams and the organisation to learn.

Thomas Edison only succeeded in creating a light bulb after 2,000 attempts. On remarking to a colleague that he had tried 2,000 times, the colleague asked if he wasn't depressed after 'failing' 2,000 times. Edison reportedly smiled and said on the contrary, he had learned over 2,000 ways not to make a light bulb.

Sadly, in the highly politicised world of the NHS, 'failure' is punishable in the most public of ways. The letter all CEOs receive to recognise their accountable officer status is a stark reminder: 'When I deem you no longer fit for purpose this will be removed from you.' The fear of failure, of reprisal, often prevents us and those around us from taking risks, from being creative, from true learning. We want staff to both be creative yet show proper judgement, not recognising the inherent contradiction.

Judgement is the rational, logical interpretation of the facts. Creativity is the irrational, illogical interpretation of the facts. They are mutually exclusive. It is about making the space at the right time to be creative and to learn that is crucial. At the operating table, with a difficult case, is not the time you want your surgeon to be creative; a leadership event or improvement time-out is!

Learning is emergent. It takes time. The rewards may not be obvious or immediate. How does the Executive Team learn together? Are your regular 1:1s transactional, or do you create space to talk about learning with your direct reports? Do you role model reflective practice? I have a series of questions I ask myself once a week. I am a great believer in the principle of 'if you think it – ink it'. I look back at my own learning journey in some disbelief. How gracious my team have been, how patient the Board, how forgiving the organisation. Every day is a school day, and it is like that for all your team – the Divisional Clinical Directors, every one of us. I'm well aware of my own failing in writing people off too early, of expecting instant results. It may seem costly, in terms of both time and money, to pull key people out for away days, planning time, team-time, but the payback is huge.

We need to build our systems and processes with space to learn. I went to visit a world class manufacturer of cars a few months ago. They have a policy in place that they do not promote someone until they have trained them and the individual demonstrates, in their current job, that they have assimilated the learning and so can perform at a higher level. Contrast that with how we usually work. We see someone with potential, promote them with a promise to support and train them, throw them into their new role and watch them struggle. Sounds familiar? The investment in making space to learn should always come up front.

Space to grow

How do you transform the learning into growth? What investment have you made into creating organisational memory? Do you have someone heading up your organisational development who has trained and practised in OD? It needs to be an exceptional individual who heads an exceptional team if you want to see real organisational growth. It is an area in which we consistently under-invest. I am talking about far more than training officers or a training department. What is your knowledge management strategy? Who holds the Executive Team to account for their development and growth? Good organisations plough 4% or more of their turnover into developing and growing their talent. Does your organisation have a talent management strategy? Growth is not linear; not always predictable. Growth may mean going backwards at times and having to unlearn things to make progress.

One of the most effective ways to grow is through coaching. Coaching is about unlocking potential, enabling individuals to examine choices and the consequences of those choices. It is about exploring identity and personal constructs. It is reflective, it is always challenging and it is about growing as an individual. Coaching is one of the most powerful interventions. Do you as a leader have a coach? Do you model coaching behaviour in your team, with colleagues, in meetings? My executive team have coaches; I have a coach. We are introducing a coaching programme over the next three years in the organisation so that everyone in a leadership role will be able to access a coach.

Coaching takes time; it is about building the capacity to self-coach and coach others. It seems quicker just to solve the problems and to give solutions but ultimately what endures and what is more effective is to give individuals the ability to grow to develop, to solve today's problems so they will be better equipped for the problems of tomorrow. Are you as a leader committed to growing the intelligence of the organisation, to that of your team, your Board, yourself? There are seven types of intelligence: linguistic, mathematical, musical, kinaesthetic, spatial, emotional and social. Is your team balanced? Do you pay enough attention to the collective needs to grow? Do you as leader truly value diversity and the different ways that people think?

I vividly remember my eldest daughter, up until the time she was about three, every night when I put her to bed, after stories and prayers, she would kiss me goodnight and as I stood up to leave she would say. 'Switch the dark on, Daddy.' In her world you pressed a switch and the dark came on. It was a sad day when she first asked me to turn the light off. We make sense of our world through the models, metaphors and paradigms we hold. We grow as we share with each other our personal models, the metaphors that give life and our constructs and paradigms that shape the way we behave. The leader must invest time and money in working with the Executive, with the Board in making space to grow.

We regularly take time after Board meetings to do a 'six-hat' review using de Bono's thinking hats to measure our growth. As an Executive, we have 6 away days a year where we review our values and behaviours, set goals/objectives for the team, look at what is working and what we could do better, speak what has been left unsaid and ensure we appreciate what each of us contributes.

In the organisation we have structured Before Action Reviews and After Action Reviews where key people get together before new projects and after each significant event to share learning and enable the organisation to develop and grow.

Each of our Divisions has a quarterly performance review with the whole Executive team. It is a structured scored assessment in six domains with evidence required. The Divisional team score themselves, the Executive team score the Division, and we agree a final score. The cumulative total leads to a rating: one of low, medium or high intensity or 'special measures'. Depending on their rating is the earned autonomy. Over the last two years there has been significant growth in approach, attitude, performance and delivery in every Division.

We have a Board Assessment Framework to assess quarterly our growth and performance. Twice a year every speciality is assessed against a matrix and reviewed by the Board. Corporate Services are rated by the Divisions on the services they provide, twice a year. All of this intelligence helps us to continuously adapt and shape the way we work, to improve, to change, to growth.

Space for the journey

Making the right spaces takes time, patience and endurance. It is a marathon, not a sprint. Yet we live in a society of instant gratification, immediate fixes. We don't want to wait any more. Instant food, instant service, an instant 'high'. Expectations in health have never been higher, from politicians and service users, Boards, shareholders, staff, leaders, partners ...

However, the journey I describe here takes a number of years. We have a 5-year vision. We have taken the first steps on the way. There is much still to do, much to learn, much will go wrong; there will be many efforts, both overt and covert, to deflect, deter and distract us from the path. How, as a leader, can you make space for the journey? The average tenure of a CEO is 2.4 years. Some unpublished figures in 2004 showed that for a first-time CEO, 50% had gone within the first year. I spoke to a colleague recently who was the ninth Chief Executive in 2 years. One Trust in Yorkshire has had nine CEOs in ten years.

The journey needs constancy, continuity and commitment. I recommend 'Mastery' by George Leonard as a cracking read for those who balk at the journey ahead. He lays out five steps that will enable the path to Mastery to be successful. I draw your attention to his third step – Intentionality. Being deliberate in everything you do; never do anything in a meaningless fashion, carelessly, without thought.

The top athletes of our time always have an intention. Tiger Woods has a deliberate plan and visualisation for each and every shot. Roger Federer never just returns a ball; each shot is crafted and executed for a reason. That's the role of the leader – to act with intentionality. It is the essence of making spaces.

If our job as leaders is to place ladders for people and organisations to move onwards and upwards, then we can best achieve this by paying attention to the spaces in between. Step wisely, step carefully, and enjoy the journey. ...

December 2007

I read the note again. 'I have to talk to you about how my father died. The Chief Executive should know these things.' I was waiting for Doug to arrive. That familiar sense of foreboding in my stomach. Another failure. I'd been CEO for three weeks – I was about to receive another lesson.

Doug didn't just walk into my room; he 'landed'. He was a giant of a man, an earth shaker! Shaking his hand was like running into a granite wall. No pleasantries, he launched into his story ..... 'It's like this,' he began.

Doug's dad was apparently, like Doug, larger than life, a character, everyone loved him – 'but the cancer got him'. Doug was 56, his dad 78. He wasted away. Towards the end the nursing home sent him to hospital. Sent him to die in a ward just before Christmas.

Doug lived in Leicester. Every night for nearly three weeks, after work, Doug would drive the 100-odd miles to spend time 'with my Da' before driving the long, lonely journey home. 'I knew the end was coming,' Doug said. A large, fat, solitary tear ran down his cheek, dripped off this chin unnoticed and splashed into his coffee.

Then 'last Friday, I'd just got in and made a drink when the phone rang...'. Doug was exhausted. It was freezing out; the roads were icy, fog in the air. It was the nurse calling. 'We think your Dad is going to slip away,' she said. 'Would you like to come back?' Doug began to sob. He knew he couldn't get back; he felt so useless that he'd failed his 'Da'. As he explained to the nurse, guilt weighed heavily on his shoulders. Then she spoke these words:

'Would you mind if I sat and held his hand till the end?'

Doug sat and wept, his giant frame shaking. 'I cannot thank her enough. I feel so bad I wasn't there but I know my Da wasn't on his own. That makes all the difference.'

I met with Janet – shy, gentle, humble Janet. 'I just did what was right,' she said. 'It was nothing special.'

*Ah, but Janet knew the secret. A secret we all as leaders have to learn. We can place many ladders. We can create many spaces, but we should always, always, **always**, make the space to care.*

References

Cooperrider, D. (1990) Positive image, positive action: the affirmative basis of organising. In: Srivastva, S. & Cooperrider, D. (eds) *Appreciative Management and Leadership: The Power of Positive Thought and Action in Organisations.* San Francisco: Jossey-Bass.

Leonard, G. (1991) *Mastery: The Keys to Success and Long-term Fulfilment.* Mass: E.P Dutton/Penguin.

4

JOURNEYING THROUGH LEADERSHIP

Judith Griffin

I n one sense, Placing Ladders could be seen to be about journeying and in this chapter, I want to reflect on what it has meant for me to be on such a journey. Metaphorically speaking, some ladders can take a long time to climb and others much quicker. My own ladder or journey in the NHS has spanned some 38 years, starting as a pre-nurse cadet to now enjoying and relishing being in my third Chief Executive post. It has been a journey that has offered me a lot to reflect on.

Whether as leaders, managers or followers, whether as a small team, large team, department, directorate or organisation, we are in the NHS because we care and the art of caring, the feeling, nurturing and supportive dimensions of our behaviour are plenty. But journeying through leadership also means that from time to time we are confronted by testing and challenging issues which require us to use our judgement and character to do the right things, in the interest of those who we care for, our colleagues, our organisation and paymasters.

In this story, I want to reflect on one aspect of the learning I have derived from my leadership experiences. The roles I have held have been diverse and I have been fortunate to have worked in organisations ranging from Acute and Mental Health Trusts to PCTs, a senior role at the Department of Health and, currently in an exciting joint appointment between the PCT and Borough Council in Blackburn with Darwen. All have provided a wide range of learning and insight and, above all, I have been privileged to have worked with some amazing and very able colleagues.

However, for the greater part of this chapter I want to focus on some of the issues from which I have learnt a great deal which are not often discussed. These reflections are not meant to be negative or a focus on testing or difficult instances but I want to use them to share with colleagues the fact that such situations occur and to acknowledge that they need to be managed on the same consistent bases of care, judgement and character.

I have been very fortunate in most of my life experiences but there are situations that shape us and inform our personal development and growth at different stages of our life and careers. These influences are often not recognised at the time but only through the passage of time. With hindsight, I now see early influences that have shaped my values and approach as a leader.

One example is from childhood where I was the eldest of five children. One of my sisters was severely disabled from birth but so much part of the 'family', we did not make much allowance – but other people did and I remember the occasions when strangers would stop and stare at someone who was 'not like us'. These early experiences of feeling what it means to be different and needing to care for others and to challenge prejudice have influenced and shaped my career path through wanting to 'make a difference' and improve things for others.

However, as I embarked on nurse training in the early 1970s, my career prospects were not promising as I had been a 'rebellious' teenager, leaving school with few academic qualifications and no aspiration other than a determination of doing a good job in caring for patients.

Luckily, others clearly recognised some potential and encouraged me or gave me opportunities; they 'placed ladders' that led to steady progressions into roles ranging from senior clinical leadership (Clinical Director and Director of Nursing), to Business Management and Performance Management and, more latterly, as Chief Executive. Their example is one that I now try to emulate through spotting and supporting talent. Doing so gives me a great sense of achievement but is not what I want to concentrate on in this story.

As a leader, one of the most important attributes is being prepared to take difficult decisions and to 'stand up and be counted' when things are tough or perhaps unpopular. In such circumstances, we seek the support of colleagues at work, the advice of experts and the encouragement of family and friends. Ultimately, however, it is our inner beliefs, values and resilience that not only guide us through difficult times but are also the ways by which others view and appreciate or judge us.

I have known many good leaders who sell their vision, engage staff and often achieve great transformation and improvement. The ones I remember, however, are the ones prepared to do the right thing in difficult circumstances and to do this in the right way – the leaders who see potential in everyone whatever their ability or background and who are prepared to 'go out on a limb' to make a difference.

These leaders demonstrate great personal integrity and resilience and are often described by the values they exhibit. I know that in my case this may be perceived as 'tough' leadership and a preparedness to take on challenges or to take difficult decisions. I hope there is also recognition of someone who is prepared to own problems and seek solutions whilst focused on the need to care and look after others, whether members of staff, patients or the wider public.

In an NHS that rightly prides itself on fairness and equity, it is evident that as leaders at all levels – Ward Managers to Chief Executives – we need to constantly and consistently live by the values that most probably brought us into the NHS in the first place. This applies to every leader (and member of staff) but, despite excellent policies and guidance and good management practice, we will all recognise occasions when we avoid difficult situations, turn a 'blind eye' or are even personally subject to unacceptable behaviour from others. Sometimes this happens through ignorance or 'not knowing what we don't know' and can generate poor practice or even discrimination.

The leader I aspire to be or the leaders I want to work with are the ones who I feel are 'authentic', who will give constructive and sometimes difficult feedback but who are fair and consistent, demonstrating a style of ethical behaviour that are centred on doing the right thing for the right reason. To illustrate this I want to share a number of reflections that were significant steps on my own career ladder

The first happened some years ago when I was appointed into a senior post with a line manager who was widely recognised as unreasonable – this however was an understatement. For the first and only time in my career, those 12 months were marked by an intolerable and unacceptable degree of bullying and harassment from my line manager. As in any similar situation, things move forward in stages and, starting from a position of trying to make things work and using mediation and other accepted practice, it was soon evident that this was not going to work. Significant senior colleagues supported me in seeing the problem was with the bully, but I needed to resolve the situation and find the solution. My first instinct was to 'fight back' in a similar fashion but this was not going to work. Therefore, first and foremost I made my position clear to the bully advising them that their behaviour was unacceptable and demonstrated I was not intimidated. I then made sure that we managed our working relationship 'by the book' ensuring that I had clear objectives and that I delivered these on all fronts. This approach disempowered the bully and I moved forward with a sense of right and determination knowing that we should never feel intimidated when we are motivated by the right things and are doing our best. Similarly, we should never abuse our 'positional power'.

Conversely, I am struck by the number of very effective and able senior colleagues who appear to avoid tackling performance issues in the staff they are line managing. This issue is one that the managers and leaders I mentor or coach often find difficult but one that is an essential responsibility of leadership at all levels. Expanding on this, I recall a senior manager whom I line managed. This person had held the same senior position for many years but when I joined the organisation it was clear that, whilst there had been performance concerns for some time, these had not previously been addressed or even raised with the individual. The individual therefore had little insight into the performance concerns and, whilst a well-liked member of the team, their contribution was often questioned or overlooked by colleagues. Consequently, they lacked the respect that should have been expected.

In normal circumstances, we all prefer to give positive encouragement and to support colleagues to succeed and this is my own preferred approach. However, in this case the senior manager concerned had not been set objectives nor had performance concerns identified and the organisation was not achieving the results required in the area for which the individual was responsible. This situation therefore required action and over a period of 6 months we put in place a performance management process which enabled the senior manager concerned to receive developmental and coaching support whilst at the same time being set clear delivery objectives. Unfortunately, the individual concerned, having not previously been subject to constructive, albeit difficult, feedback, found the process difficult, could only see the negatives, and eventually left the organisation.

What we expect is that in taking action this will be done with empathy and care whilst following processes that are set out in good HR practices. In other words, doing the right thing and doing it in the right way. In this particular example I personally struggled as I could see the difficulties the individual concerned was experiencing. However, using personal reflection and seeking confirmation from senior colleagues that my approach was fair and necessary, I felt that I stayed true to personal values and a code of practice that I would expect to receive myself. By not dealing with difficult performance issues, the previous line manager had let down the individual, the wider team and essentially the patients for whom the organisation was responsible. It also exposed the leader, as others perceived the lack of action as a failure.

Not long after this experience, I took up post as Chief Executive of a large specialist Mental Health Trust, a career move that on reflection has had the most significant personal impact on me as a leader. Putting some context on this I had at this stage 30 years' experience in the NHS where I had provided professional leadership to Mental Health nurses, commissioned Mental Health Services and performance managed Mental Health organisations. Nevertheless, until then I had no idea of the extent of the stigma and discrimination that is so prevalent against people with mental illness (and often to staff who work in the field of mental health). I had no real understanding of the inequalities faced by people with mental illness and their carers and I have to admit that my ignorance until then probably made me culpable by not taking the time to understand the situation and to then use my position of influence to make a difference and to challenge discrimination.

With knowledge comes responsibility, and I was determined to achieve transformation and improvement for service users based on principles of recovery, hope and equality. Over a period of 18 months, service users and carers were involved with senior and experienced clinicians and managers in developing groundbreaking proposals to introduce new and enhanced service models that would make a real difference to people's lives and experience of mental health services.. However, in places, local people and colleagues in positions of influence in partner organisations opposed the changes. This is familiar territory for any senior manager or leader who is trying to introduce change and the usual processes of consultation and engagement were utilised throughout. I was struck, however, by the similarity to the example above on bullying insofar that the nature of the opposition was essentially personal and discriminatory based on fear and ignorance about mental illness. Moreover, the resistance came from people who should have taken responsibility for achieving improvement but at that stage did not 'own' the problem and therefore were unhappy with the proposed solution!

As the leader of the organisation I inevitably needed to 'front' the arguments for change and, as well as using a factual and considered approach setting out the benefits and risks, it was the use of stories that both motivated me and my colleagues to provide the most powerful approach to counteract opposition: standing up, challenging stigma and ignorance, and doing it well by use of facts and information, using stories of what it is like to live with mental illness and being a voice for people who are disadvantaged. This is a positive use of 'positional power' and is a profound move forward for leaders at all levels within the organisation and one which I learnt from based on the experience of working in a mental health organisation. The important lesson is of being prepared to speak out with passion for the things that matter. This is the purpose for which we chose to work in the NHS but which often gets lost in how we think about our roles.

We often describe our role through our objectives and the targets we need to meet. We use policies to guide us in best practice and inevitably do our best and hopefully succeed knowing we have done a good job by the external and objective measures that are essential in a 'world class' organisation. These, however, are still only management tools and approaches but I know there are people who may be embarrassed to use words that demonstrate emotional abilities of involvement and engagement. Goleman's work on 'emotional intelligence' is informative and I will come back to this at the end of this chapter. But we can see strong resonance of his ideas as the core Personal *Skills* of the *Leadership Quality Framework* as was developed by the Leadership Centre of the then Modernisation Agency and is now still very much at the core of leadership development work of the Institute of Improvement and Innovation. Their inclusion here is to reinforce them as key aspects of the inter-personal dimensions of behaviours that are central to our everyday work:

Personal Skills: Leadership Quality Framework

Self belief

Outstanding leaders maintain a positive 'can do' sense of confidence which enables them to be shapers rather than followers, even in the face of opposition. This prime personal quality is built upon success and learning in a broad range of varied situations over time.

Features of this quality include:
- Relishing a challenge.
- Being prepared to stand up for what they believe in.
- Working beyond the call of duty, when this is required.
- Speaking up if this is needed. In doing so, their integrity and their motivation for service improvement will sustain them.

Self awareness

Outstanding leaders have a high degree of self awareness. They know their own strengths and limitations, and they use failure or misjudgement as an opportunity for learning.

Features of this quality include:
- Being aware of their own emotions.
- Being aware of their personal impact on others, particularly when they are under pressure as they have an understanding of the 'triggers' to which they are susceptible.

Self management

Outstanding leaders are able to pace themselves, staying for the long haul when necessary. Self management, supported by emotional self awareness, enables them to regulate their behaviour, even when provoked.

Features of this quality include:
- Being tenacious and resilient in the face of difficulty.
- Being able to cope with an increasingly complex environment – with the blurring of organisational boundaries and the requirement to work in partnership across the health and social care context.

Drive for improvement

Outstanding leaders are motivated by wanting to make a real difference to people's health by delivering a high quality service and by developing improvements to service.

Features of this quality include:
- A deep sense of vocation for public service driven by an identification with the needs of patients and service users.

- A primary focus on achievement of goals for the greater good of others, and not the leader's own reputation.
- Investing their energy in bringing about health improvements – even to the extent of wanting to leave a legacy which is about effective partnership, inter-agency working and community involvement.

Personal integrity

There is much at stake in leading health services. Outstanding leaders bring a sense of integrity to what they do that helps them to deliver to the best of their abilities.

Features of this quality include:

- Believing in a set of key values borne out of broad experience of, and commitment to, the service which stands them in good stead, especially when they are under pressure.
- Insistence on openness and communication, motivated by values about inclusiveness and getting on with the job.
- Acting as a role model for public involvement and the dialogue that all staff, including the front line, need to have with service users.
- Resilience that enables them to push harder, when necessary, in the interests of developing or improving the service.

www.NHSLeadershipQualities.nhs.uk

The above, together with other key qualities including 'empowering others', as well as working collaboratively in teams and with others, are dimensions of inter-personal behaviour that are vital to us being 'who we are' and being authentic. Once we start to say what we are about and to understand our common purpose, we become a movement for change and transformation. This is the purpose or 'glue' that binds us together.

If anything, we are sometimes reluctant to use these skills. As a minor case in point, in NHS Blackburn with Darwen we hold regular workshops that involve every member of staff in the commissioning part of my current organisation, ranging from front-line administrative staff to Commissioning Managers and Executive Directors. At one of the first of these, I asked staff as they arrived to write down on a Post-it note what their job was. With few exceptions, everyone wrote down their job title, sometimes with a few lines of commentary. Throughout most of my career this is what I would have done because it is easy and this is what we think our leaders expect.

But no more. As Chief Executive I have made my purpose (my job) clear which is to improve the health and wellbeing of everyone who lives in Blackburn with Darwen – a privilege and responsibility of which I am proud, albeit sometimes also daunted.

Fortunately, I am not alone and now every single member of staff and our partners share this common purpose and are preparing to take a step change in how we work and deliver improvement for local people. With this focus we can push back resistance and introduce innovation exampled in Blackburn with Darwen by the joint commitment between the PCT and Local Authority to 'Re:fresh', a unique initiative to provide free access to physical activities and health trainers for everyone in the Borough.

I recognise that for much of my career I have delivered and done a good job, met objectives and often, I hope, made a real difference and improved services, always trying to do this in the right way and for the right reasons. I wish, however, that I had realised at an earlier stage the power of speaking with passion and telling the story that matters – one of optimism, hope and determination – because if we don't deliver there is no one waiting in the wings to take up the challenge. We, all of us, have to stand up and be counted to take responsibility for our own behaviours and always care for others – even when challenged or needing to take tough decisions.

All leaders have a great privilege that brings great responsibility: to speak with passion and lead with purpose; to empower staff to take forward change and transformation where this will achieve improvement; and to stand up for those who are subject to discrimination, inequality or bullying.

In the wider world and since the Enron fiasco and other similar situations, the theme of 'Ethical Leadership' (Connock & Johns 1995, amongst others) has attracted much more attention. The common emphasis on honesty, transparency and behaving morally has been given added impetus. Being direct, straightforward and open in dealings with others were regularly identified as key elements in managing ethically. At its simplest level it is about doing unto others as you would have them do unto you which was a key response to ideas of ethical leadership identified in a survey of middle managers carried out by Archie Carrol in 1990 as discussed in Connock & Johns (op. cit.).

In his book entitled *The Connected Leader*, Emmanuel Gobillot (2007) has posed a set of key issues which has relevance for us all. He proposes that we should all be able to reflect on the tenets that:

- There must (always) be a better way to lead;
- There must (always) be a better way to engage an organisation's creativity, passion and drive;
- There must (always) be a better way to relate to (others).

His assertion, that we all have a need to grow and find meaning as the driver of engagement is both timely and pointed and can serve us all well. And so back to Goleman and his colleagues whose work on 'emotional intelligence' has brought to the fore the importance of the interpersonal to discussions of the work of leaders and leadership. For Goleman *et al.* (1998) the emotional intelligence competencies are categorised as:

- Personal competencies:
  - Self-awareness
  - Self-management
- Social competencies:
  - Social awareness
  - Relationship management.

These are not innate talents but are learnt and they serve a key role at making us more 'resonant' and thus more effective. In summary, the more we practise these competencies, the better we become.

Reading through these reflections has strengthened my own resolve and quest to focus on the whole picture – to use the whole range of tools in the box, the here and now as well as the long term, the popular and the unpopular, and on being prepared to act to make a difference for improvement in the quality of service and care for the public. Finally, there is one major lesson that draws this together and that is I wish I had recognised earlier in my career – the need to tell the story and to talk from the heart. Looking back, I believe that for the majority of my career I have done a good job. I regret, though, that it was not until the past 5 years or so that I have felt comfortable in sharing experiences of this kind.

References

NHSIII: Leadership Qualities Framework. www.NHSleadershipQualities.nhs.uk.

Goleman, D. *et al.* (1998) *Working with Emotional Intelligence.* London: Bloomsbury.

Connock, S. & Johns, T. (1985) *Ethical Leadership.* London: IPD.

Connock, A.B. (1990) *Business and Society: Ethics and Stakeholder Management.* SWC.

Gobillot, E. (2007) *The Connected leader: Creating Agile Organisations for People, Performance and Profit.* London: Kogan Page.

5

LEADING WITH PASSION:
PLACING LADDERS FAR AND WIDE

Caroline Shaw

There is something about people who are passionate. All of us have met them in our personal and working lives. Typically they speak with conviction and belief. They look you in the eye when face to face. And when you hear them talk they leave you feeling stronger in your own desire to do something to make a difference, just as much as you see them doing in their everyday actions. The role of the leader is also about engaging people so that they can develop a deeper connection to their work and as a consequence become more passionate themselves. Leading with passion; placing ladders far and wide is something that I have experienced from both sides. It is something that I have tried to practise in my working life and it is now the focus of my contribution to this book of readings.

When I was young

To begin with though, I feel that it is important to start this chapter by sharing my story with you. I am from Kendal in the North West of England. I was born in 1967 in Helmchase Maternity Hospital and grew up in a beautiful rural community. I love the Lake District, the lifestyle and its people and go back every month to visit my mother and my many close friends there. My father had a chronic illness when I was young and therefore had an ongoing need of NHS services. Seeing how the NHS provided care and treatment to my father really opened my eyes. I quickly understood the importance of health services and the provision of care.

From babies to boards

I first joined the NHS as a midwife because I wanted to work with people in a meaningful way – and you can't get much more meaningful than helping to bring a baby into the world. There is a story about Socrates who, when asked which of his two parents he liked more, retorted that his father as a sculptor made many beautiful things to admire, but he preferred his mother who, as a midwife, was able to help to bring forth new-borns into the world who created their own lives. I did my nurse training at Blackpool Victoria Hospital and my midwifery training at Leicester Royal Infirmary.

It was when I began practising as a midwife that I became interested in thinking beyond what I was doing and started to look at ways to provide a bit more for patients in terms of choice, control and continuity. A good example of this was offering women home births with the same midwife with whom they had built up a relationship throughout their pregnancy.

I loved working as a midwife, but knew that I could make an even greater difference to healthcare by moving into NHS management. So, always valuing the benefit of education, I undertook further qualifications – a first degree in Health Studies at De Montford University in Leicester and later a Master of Science in Health Policy and Management at Birmingham University. After a number of managerial roles in hospitals in Leicestershire, I moved to Manchester in 2002 to become Deputy Chief Executive and Executive Director of Operations at the University Hospital of South Manchester Foundation Trust. I was part of the executive team responsible for taking the Trust from zero to three star status in one year – winning the 2004 Health Service Journal award for improvement in performance management and, as a result, the Secretary of State's commendation for health care management.

Ladders and leading

As is the case for many of us, there are a number of people who have placed important ladders over my career. The two people from whom I learned the most are Dr Helen Bevan, Director of Service Transformation at the NHS Institute for Innovation and Improvement, and Dr Peter Homa, Chief Executive of Nottingham University Hospitals NHS Trust. I worked with Helen on the re-engineering programme in Leicester in the early '90s and she showed me the importance of methodology such as Lean and service line management. Peter was an inspirational leader and excellent role model.

I was appointed Chief Executive of The Christie in September 2005 – one of Europe's leading cancer centres. I am proud to have moved rapidly up the career ladder since joining the NHS as a midwife 22 years ago to become one of the youngest female Chief Executives in the NHS. And I have been fortunate to have worked with a team of very able people. Together we have successfully led award-winning teams and have developed a strong track record of improving patient care through reform and modernisation. Passion and determination are the two key ingredients to this success: passion for what we wanted to do, and the determination to achieve it. In so doing have created a culture in which people are:

- becoming more engaged and connected with our organisation
- becoming better performers and at higher levels
- enabling and supporting others to perform well
- promoting the organisation regionally, nationally and internationally
- delivering exceptional standards and care.

We all need to learn from others as well as from ourselves. I have always had many different role models – from my mother, to famous women leaders, to amazingly successful entrepreneurs. When I was training as a midwife, I saw female gynaecologists modify their behaviour to be like male colleagues, but I have always been very conscious never to do that. I am proud to be a woman.

Enthusiasm and encouragement

My experience and learning has taught me that leadership is a combination of strategy and character. I always aim to be myself with everyone, which is down-to-earth, friendly, enthusiastic but focused on the job in hand. I invest time and effort in developing relationships with key people and believe that it's always the old fashioned approach that works best – talking to them face-to-face. You manage things, but you lead people. In order to influence people I try to stand in their shoes and understand the issue from their side. Only then can I know what will motivate or convince them. There's an art and a science to influencing people. They are persuaded by reason, but moved by emotion. I have learnt that people who demonstrate intellectual and emotional connection to their work typify an enthusiasm that leads to better outcomes and flow. We need to ensure that our staff and teams are engaged in meaningful work that meets their intellectual needs of achievement, autonomy and mastery. But their emotional needs are equally important including purpose, affiliation and appreciation. I make time to see the issues that affect our people in their own contexts. Spending a day working in our hospital kitchen helped me to appreciate basic things such as the choice of menu for our patients. When we are making difficult decisions around managing costs and value, it's important we understand exactly what it is our staff and patients don't want to lose.

My job as Chief Executive is to remain the 'helicopter' in the organisation and always see the bigger picture. The very essence of leadership is to have vision. It is my job to ensure that everything fits into the big strategic picture. I need to ensure that, even though people are focused on their particular area of responsibility, they also understand the bigger picture and where and how they fit into and contribute to it. People in an organisation need responsibility and accountability to thrive and blossom. The challenge is to select the very best people to do what you want done, and have self-restraint to keep from meddling with them while they do it. We shouldn't tell people how to do things, but tell them what to do and let them impress us with their results. Our staff know I'm there to provide guidance and support, but I often say to them: 'Don't come to me with the problem, but the solution to the problem.'

Being strong and being seen

Coming to The Christie has enabled me to implement new ways of working and managing. I implemented a new clinical and managerial structure which gave a lot more responsibility and accountability to divisions and teams – especially clinical leaders. Service line management and balanced scorecards have been introduced, with 360° appraisals and bespoke development programmes to help develop staff. Their excellent performance results have been the 'proof in the pudding'. But people need to know they have a strong leader who will battle for them and take risks. Being willing to make decisions is perhaps the most important quality in a good leader. Many staff think that I am a hard task master, with high expectations, but they also know that I am committed, driven and will fight in their corner when the pressure is on. The ultimate measure of a leader is not how we act in moments of comfort, but how we act at times of challenge and controversy.

A chief executive needs to be visible and 'seen' within the organisation. I regularly do walkabouts, not just to the usual places at the usual times, but when night nurses have just started their shifts and in the backroom offices. When I first joined The Christie, I spent time working in our teenage cancer unit as a 'jobbing nurse' and other areas, not just to highlight that every job plays an important part in the organisation, but to understand the motivations, issues etc. from different groups of staff. I also always try to ensure that I present the monthly team briefing, staff induction, and attend other staff events. I also believe that a high-profile chief executive can build confidence and pride in staff and think it's important to feature in PR and publicity material and events and undertake media interviews.

All these tactics have helped implement an ambitious five-year strategy which breaks new ground and is set to transform treatment and care for cancer patients. A £72 million investment plan over the next two years includes a new £35 million patient treatment centre, which will include the largest early clinical trials unit in the world – and a unique network of £17 million Christie radiotherapy centres in other parts of the area to deliver treatment closer to people's homes.

A leader's work is also about looking beyond the organisation. Working with a wide range of partners, we have been able to establish the nationally applauded *Manchester Versus Cancer* alliance to improve the early diagnosis of cancer, and helped launch the Manchester Cancer Research Centre in partnership with The University of Manchester and Cancer Research UK.

At whatever level we are in the organisation, it is vital that we never forget about 'passion' and 'determination': passion for what you want to do and determination to achieve it. A 'do it' attitude should never be underestimated; it's about having energy to reinvigorate people. In our busy day-to-day working lives, it is useful to have uppermost in our minds what we are working towards. A simple tool we adopted at The Christie was to introduce value cards for all staff so everyone has a constant reminder about what it's all about and what we are all here for. The value cards are based on staff and patients' views and focus on 'pride' in the job and our organisation.

It's personal

It is also important that our own personal values ,as leaders are made explicit and that we stay true to these. We need to use our heads and our hearts. If people are not engaged in something, it is less likely that change will follow. We should never lose sight of the core values of the NHS, of which we should be really proud.

As leaders we should also be able to assess our own strengths and weaknesses and to make use of the expertise of our colleagues. To use football managers as an analogy, whilst I am definitely more of an Alex Ferguson than an Arsene Wenger, I do have the flexibility to change my style to encourage development and ambition. We need also to demonstrate trust in others and make our role more facilitative. My current role is now 70% external facing. It's easier to be a dictator, but I have had to let go without taking my eye off the ball.

I have also valued and been receptive to the learning that is available around us. I have taken inspiration and advice from everyone around me and beyond. Role models are important, not so we can be like them, but to take learning points from them. I have many role models: Madonna, for reinventing herself time and time again, and not staying with one static plan. JK Rowling for being single-minded. She knew she had a writing talent, and when she was unemployed, she took the courage to write her first Harry Potter novel. Nigella Lawson, the cookery writer and presenter, inspires me to stay true to myself and be proud of being a female and feminine. I am proud to walk into our boardroom in a skirt and heels, as I know I'll be respected and listened to in a skirt or a suit. And runner Paula Radcliffe inspires me to work hard to succeed, no matter what obstacles are put in my way. My role models are not just high-profile either. My mum has inspired me to 'believe in what you do' and to 'regret nothing' and I follow this advice every day.

As a leader I place great emphasis on personal relationships. The ability to connect and build strong and effective relationships with people is critical to success – especially with senior staff. We need to see and be seen across the organisation. We need to show an interest in people, invest time and energy in talking to them and not be shy about asking personal questions when it's appropriate. In my early management career I kept a book about GP fundholders which had written down their children's names, favourite footballs team, etc. I would always make sure I remembered this information before each meeting. We should admit to not knowing, get back to people and be decisive. People will have more respect if you make a decision, even if it's not the decision they were hoping for, than if you won't make one.

Above all we should listen to our patients and understand their experiences. They are at the heart of everything we do and the very reason why we should be placing ladders far and wide.

6

LEADERSHIP THROUGH CONNECTION: ENABLING DISTRIBUTED LEADERSHIP

Leigh Griffin

'You're better than no one, and no one is better than you.'

Dylan, 'To Ramona', 1965

In the preface of their book, *The New Leaders*, Goleman, Boyatiz & McKee (2002) told a short story about Mark Loehr, the CEO of Sound View Technology, a technology company in Connecticut which had a small number of friends, colleagues and family members who were lost in the September 11 tragedy.

On hearing of the news, Loehr's first response was to invite employees to come to the office the next day 'not to work, but to share their feelings and talk over what to do'. Over the following days, Loehr was there to console, to support and to share in the loss of his colleagues. Every night at 9.45pm, he sent out an e-mail to the entire company about the personal side of ongoing events. Loehr encouraged and guided conversations to help to make sense and find meaning in the chaos and loss. Employees were actively encouraged to compile a memory book to share thoughts, feeling, fears and hopes.

In crises, threats, key challenges, difficulties and setbacks, people look to their leaders for emotional guidance and to create opportunities for sense-making and meaning. Loehr was able to attune and enable others to connect and engage in action that resonated with their feelings.

Using the Loehr story, Goleman and his colleagues then posed a question:

'What would our lives look like if the organisations where we spent our working days were naturally places of resonance, with leaders who inspired us? ... Imagine what an organisation would look like if the concept of resonant leadership was a founding principle, rather than (as usually the case) a corrective [reaction].'

My starting point as such is that leaders of health care organisations are in positions of authority, responsibility and privilege. As Goleman *et al.* observed, in organisations:

'there are many leaders, not just one, as leadership is distributed ... it resides in every person at every level who in one way or other acts as leader to a group of followers.'

They have, however, to earn and sustain the respect of their managers and wider workforce and, in doing this, should always keep in mind the interdependence of all parts of the organisation. 'As there are many leaders, so will there be a variety of styles and approaches.' But, through an open and democratic approach and an affiliative style, co-production and co-ownership of change can best be secured, owned and sustained to make a difference for those we are here to serve.

Through my 7 years as an NHS Chief Executive, I have steadily come to realise and appreciate the value and benefit of connectivity. The work of the leader is to ensure that the top is connected with the middle and bottom within the organisation and that there are mechanisms for establishing and supporting these connections. Moreover, our organisations exist within a community and it is essential that we create networks and connections with the wider community. This, in essence, reflects the importance of resonance, as set out by Boyatzis & McKee in *Resonant Leadership* (2005). For me placing ladders is all about strengthening connection as this will open up conversations about what is possible through collaborative involvement.

My story will focus on some of the simple steps I have taken to connect and engage with my staff and starts with when I first appointed as a Chief Executive in East Lancashire in 2002. I decided at the outset that I would create space to regularly spend time working, as an extra pair of hands, with front-line staff. This hopefully made me and my role more accessible and understood by a range of staff, and also helped me to 'ground myself' through gaining an understanding of frustrations and constraints at the front line.

Subsequently, at Morecambe Bay and most recently at Sefton, I have supplemented this approach through the hosting of regular open, informal discussion sessions held at various times and locations, and to which any member of staff is able to attend. These sessions, attended by 3–30 staff, again provide an opportunity for 'grounding' and a narrowing of the distance that can so often persist between front line staff and Chief Officers. Issues raised are handled in confidence if so wished, whilst concerns can also be separately addressed through our weekly staff briefings or bi-monthly newsletters.

Every Chief Executive is acutely aware that every statement they make and every bit of body language is open to interpretation and onward communication. The value of connectivity with front line staff, further supported by drop-in visits to workplaces, is that such connection will trigger a cascade of onward conversation, discussion and commentary – hopefully positive!

At Morecambe Bay and Sefton, I have additionally sought to demonstrate personal leadership and cultivate leadership behaviours in others through the hosting of regular wider management forums. These are whole-day events to which circa 100–120 of the organisation's senior managers and clinicians are encouraged to attend.

These events have multiple purposes. Again, they help me to connect. But they also promote cross-organisational understanding and working, helping to counter any 'silo' tendencies. Most critically, however, I have used them in Sefton to set out my beliefs and values, to raise debate about strategic aims and direction and to actively engage with others in co-creating a vision that will drive cultural change to impact on standards and service improvement. It was also a fundamental basis for developing and sustaining distributive leadership.

NHS Sefton is a PCT constructed through organisational change in 2006, replacing two precedent PCTs which, despite prior histories of Sefton-wide working, had profoundly different management styles, cultures, relationships and financial health. Faced with a strong degree of 'us and themism', and an understandable anxiety as to the impact of organisational change, I have convened regular Wider Management Forums since mid 2007, supported by the able facilitation of Brigid Russell and Martha Creaser and excellent in-house support.

My intent has been to demonstrate a range of leadership styles through these sessions, as set out by Goleman *et al.* (2002). I have sought to illustrate the importance of the visionary, coaching, affiliative, democratic, pacesetting and commanding styles and approaches of leadership. Ultimately, this has been based on a belief in the importance of resonance and inclusivity, where all have a voice and where self-awareness and feedback are key. In leading complex organisations with multiple professional influences and interests, the sessions also reflect Jim Collins' ideas on 'Level 5' leadership, whereby leaders operate to get things done within a diffuse power structure through a blend of personal humility and professional will (Collins, 2006).

The sessions, scheduled well in advance to enable attendance (which is 'strongly encouraged'), are held away from PCT facilities at accessible, attractive locations across Sefton (e.g. Aintree Racecourse, Southport Convention Centre). Ample time is included for networking, with a health-friendly lunchtime walk built in.

The content of the sessions initially sought to secure the right blend of presentations and discussion. Topics ranged from themed sessions on engagement (with staff and with other partners), leadership and leadership behaviours, the understanding and shaping organisational culture. These were interlaced with presentations, which regularly include 'What is going on out there?' and 'How are we doing?' sessions led by myself and updates from Directors on issues such as Strategic Aims and Directions and Commissioning Assurance, leading into group work and questions and answers (q+a) involving all Directors, including the PEC Chair.

More recently, the day has been split into two. The 'stock-take' sessions and updates/discussion/q+a sessions are now concentrated in the morning, with attendees having the opportunity of choosing from a list of 5–6 masterclasses in the afternoon. These masterclasses, led by a senior manager/leader from within the PCT or, occasionally, by external experts, have included the following:

- Tackling health inequalities
- Partnership development
- Understanding and managing budgets

- Managing Performance
- Coaching skills
- Building effective teams
- Influencing and communicating
- World class information for intelligent commissioning
- Workforce planning.

The format of the days has been shaped through feedback and detailed evaluation of each session, set in the context of explicit aims – we learn by doing. The full evaluation for each event, as undertaken by Brigid Russell and Martha Creaser, is placed on the staff website within a week of each event.

Evaluation has been instrumental in helping my colleagues and I to learn from the experience of our group sessions and our designed and tailored programmes. This design additionally takes on board the views of a cross-organisational planning group of managers, and issues highlighted by my Directors and myself.

To gain the benefits of such sessions you have to give a lot of yourself. From the outset, I have sought to be clear as to my values, beliefs, ambitions, hopes and concerns, seeking challenge and views from the broader team of leaders. Initial sessions started with all participants invited to anonymously express on postcards one-word views as to how they felt the new PCT was doing, how we were perceived by partners, what frustrated managers most, etc. At the end of the day, I have fed the findings back and led a discussion as to their implications for us all. Whilst this has exposed concerns and frustrations, it has also enabled all to appreciate the wide range of perspectives, helping to shape a better understanding of perceptions and realities.

Attendance at the sessions has consistently been 80–90% of those invited. Of these, circa 70% have returned evaluation forms at the end of the day, enabling assessment across a range of issues including:

- How well did we achieve the aims of the day?
- What worked well?
- What did not work so well?
- What could we do differently next time?

and latterly:

- How did you rate the masterclass/workshop you attended?; and
- Should we continue with these sessions?

Of the above questions, the rating out of ten as to how well the aims of the day had been achieved has consistently risen, from a mean score of 6.5 (and a mode of 7) to the most recent scores of 7.3 and 7.2 (mode 8). Components which have been particularly valued have been the opportunity to network and to work in mixed groups, and group discussion, Directorate action planning on staff engagement, discussions on culture, strategic aims, corporate objectives and world class commissioning, the Chief Executive overview and, latterly and particularly strongly, the workshops on skills development.

Comments on the workshops help give a human feel to the evaluation, and include 'Subject well communicated – put in clinician's terms'; 'An excellent taster session – very thought-provoking'; 'Most valuable workshop I have attended for some time'; and 'Wish we had had more time'.

As to what hasn't worked so well, the list is (thankfully!) shorter. A number of respondents stated a wish to better relate corporate objectives to their own roles/spheres of influence; commented on the frustrations of group dynamics, where dominant voices can frustrate; cited insufficient time (although others refer to 'a long day'!); and a desire to focus more on action planning. Whilst most of the presentations have been well received, the sessions have also helped me to reflect on and develop the presentational skills of myself and my Directors.

As signalled above, the feedback received has helped to shape the design of future sessions. Initiated during my time at Morecambe Bay, I have increasingly sought to use the sessions to develop corporate understanding on organisational issues [or corporacy], particularly in the context of the profoundly changing nature of the roles and expectations of PCTs, the recent vitalisation of commissioning and the rapid development of systems management.

This has raised issues as to the appropriateness of sessions which bring together PCT commissioning and provider leaders, whilst at the same time there has been a clear internal separation of functions and a rapidly emergent appreciation of the purpose and nature of systems management rules.

The balance has to be struck between the value of PCT-wide corporacy, within which the impact of strategic aims, corporate objectives and World Class Commissioning on commissioners and providers can be discussed, and the need to treat all providers consistently from an explicit commissioning perspective.

Whilst this issue is currently under review, my personal view is that, whilst they remain the formal responsibility of the PCT, provider services managers should have the same access to leadership development as other PCT managers, albeit with sessions designed to ensure that PCT provider services do not gain an unfair insight on strategic or operational commissioning intentions. This latter aim has been supported by the emergence of complementary Provider Services management sessions, led by the PCT's Director of Provider Services, and by the PCT ensuring that its strategic and commissioning intentions are shared with all providers, and supported by a suppliers' briefing day (November 2008).

Managers are overwhelmingly keen for the Wider Management Forums to continue every 3–4 months as PCT-wide events. This will be kept under review in the context of systems management rules and guidance and the further development of Sefton's provider services.

Other issues under review are whether, in the context of strengthened joint working and potential integration of functions with Sefton Borough Council, the Forums should be recast as a joint LA/PCT initiative, and how best we can strengthen clinical influence to the Forums: whilst six of NHS Sefton's full Executive Team have a clinical background and/or current role, we still wish to strengthen the influence of clinicians, albeit within the systems management context referred to above.

What would I have done differently? Probably little, although in retrospect (the best teacher) I would have intensified the regularity of sessions at Morecambe Bay during that PCT's pre-dissolution periods and its dissemblement to four replacement bodies. I would also have initiated the sessions at Sefton earlier, using the workshops at both PCTs as a mechanism to help manage the disruptive and protracted period of organisational change.

I am also conscious that both the Staff Discussion Forums and Wider Management Forums must not become vehicles for any inappropriate emphasis on the role of the Chief Executive. The sessions are designed to enable distributive leadership, to promote networking, debate and challenge and to spread ownership rather than to concentrate attention on the Chief Officer. To help ensure this, I have consistently used feedback and evaluation to counter the risk of passive reception and to foster enquiry and challenge in designing sessions.

In doing what I am doing, I am becoming more convinced of the value and importance of connecting and engaging with all staff. This is as important as the vision and strategy thing. The work of Gronn (2000) on the concept of distributed leadership points to the value of concertive action, i.e. the aggregated effect of individuals' contribution of initiative, expertise and commitment to the organisation. He also points to the value of the openness of the boundaries of leadership. It seems to me that a key element of my work as a leader is that of creating leaders by opening doors and connecting others. Emanuel Gobillot's (2007) work points to the importance of our need to sustain engagement and involvement through dialogue, to align 'top, middle and bottom' through shared meaning and to connect through trust. Let's work together to connect even more.

'If everything seems under control, you're not going fast enough.'

Mario Andretti, ex-Formula 1 driver.

References

Boyatzis, R. & McKee, A. (2005) *Resonant Leadership: Renewing Yourself and Connecting with Others Through Mindfulness, Hope and Compassion*. Harvard Business School Press.

Collins, J. (2006) *Good to Great and the Social Sectors*. London: Random House.

Goleman, D. *et al.* (2002) *The New Leaders: Transforming the Art of Leadership into the Science of Results*. London: Little Brown.

Gobillot, E. (2007) *The Connected leader: Creating Agile Organisations for People, Performance and Profit*. London: Kogan Page.

Gronn, P. (2000) Distributed properties: a new architecture for leadership. *Administration & Leadership*, Vol. 28, No. 3, pp. 317–338.

7

LADDERS OR CLIMBING FRAME?

David Fillingham, CBE

T he title of this book is an interesting one. It conjured up in my mind's eye a gleaming staircase ascending into the clouds. Perhaps it's a metaphor for the traditional view of career development, in which ambitious young managers scramble to reach the top of their chosen career ladders?

As I have progressed in my own career, I have found that for most people, myself included, this analogy doesn't really work. In a fast-changing world, planning a career in meticulous detail and then elegantly implementing that plan, is a luxury that few can enjoy. What's more, everyone faces trials, tribulations, challenges and backward steps. I have come to see my own career not so much as a ladder but more as a climbing frame in a children's playground. The aim is to move around the frame; sometimes ascending, sometimes not; moving laterally, or even stepping down a rung or two to reach your desired goal. The ultimate satisfaction is not in getting to the top of the ladder; it's in becoming the best climber that you can be, taking interest from each part of the experience and helping others become better climbers too.

I have been immensely lucky to have lots of interesting experiences during my twenty-five-year clamber around my own career climbing frame. The early part of my career was spent in human resources and marketing positions in the manufacturing sector. After joining the NHS in 1989, I worked in almost every part of the service – at regional level, in Primary Care, at a Health Authority, in two Acute Hospitals and, for four years at the Department of Health. It certainly feels like I have been up, down and across my climbing frame, at a variety of speeds and angles!

In September 2004, I was appointed as Chief Executive of Bolton Hospital NHS Trust. Halfway through the third decade of my management career I was no longer looking for ladders to go up. Instead I took stock of my experiences so far and reflected on what more I could do to become the best climber I was capable of being. I came to see this as having three interlocking themes:

FIGURE 1: FOCUS OF EFFORT

The rest of this chapter explores each of these themes in turn.

Articulating an inspiring vision

Imagine that it is your first day in a new job. You leave home especially early to make sure you are not late for your Corporate Induction session. You arrive both nervous and excited. It's a big step for you. You don't know what your new organisation will be like to work for. Perhaps you'll even stay here for the rest of your career?

Eight hours later, you've slogged your way through a dozen lectures on Health & Safety and Fire Regulations. You feel like you have been given lots of lists of things you mustn't do. Sadly you are still not really any clearer about what your new organisation stands for, what its values are and how it is trying to make the world a better place.

All too many people in work have this experience. In my early days as a Chief Executive (clutching my newly acquired MBA), I talked a lot about strategies, plans, targets and the need for delivery. I forgot one of the basics of human nature. People need to feel that they are making a difference. They need to be moved by an inspiring vision.

In Bolton I carry out the opening session on all our Induction Days for new starters. I start by talking about the four aims of the hospital:

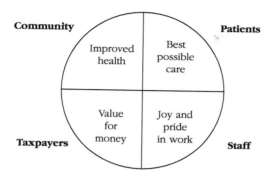

FIGURE 2: FOUR AIMS OF OUR HOSPITAL

I ask everyone present to imagine that they are coming along on their first day, not as a new member of staff but as a patient or relative. I ask them to share their personal experiences and talk about what it feels like to be on the receiving end of NHS care. Together, we then discuss how to describe what 'best possible care' would mean for each of us as a patient.

The level of energy in the room visibly rises. There are also nods of agreement when we discuss the fact that everyone present falls into each of the four categories of our aims. We all want the best care for ourselves and our families, improved health for our communities, value for the hard-earned money which we pay out in taxes and satisfying and fulfilling jobs which we can enjoy and in which we can take pride.

The process of developing this vision for Bolton Hospital took many months. It involved a wide cross-section of staff, patients and partners. We felt that getting the words right was important. This isn't something we want to change each time we rewrite the Trust Business Plan. It's something that should be an enduring set of aims.

Managers at every level in an organisation need to provide an inspiring vision for those who work for them. Patrick Lencioni in his fable entitled 'Three Signs of a Miserable Job' [1], emphasises that for work to be satisfying everyone needs 'relevance'. We need to know how we are making a difference and for whom. In Healthcare, it is particularly important that this vision should resonate with the values and ideals of those working on the front line of the service. It needs to remind them why they joined up in the first place.

The vision which we developed in Bolton is now the centrepiece of the Trust's five-year strategy and provided the framework for our integrated business plan submitted for our Foundation Trust Application. To be effective, it can't simply be a set of worthy but vague aspirations. It needs concrete focus. So we have set tangible and challenging five-year goals under each of these headings, e.g.: to reduce our hospital standardised mortality rate to below 85 against the national average of 100 (Improved Health); to cut defects in the patient care process such as cancellations or medication errors by 50% each year (Best Possible Care); to improve productivity by 10% per annum (Value For Money); and to be recognised as one of the UK's leading employers in any sector (Joy and Pride).

As Chief Executive, I try not to miss any opportunity to tell people the story behind this vision and how it relates to their day-to-day job. Whether it be in the fortnightly meetings I hold with cross-sections of staff, walkabouts around the hospital, our regular BICS (Bolton Improving Care System, of which more later) events, my email newsletters or in more formal meetings, we use the framework time and time again.

There are inevitably risks to this. Sometimes the vision is met with understandable cynicism. An overstretched nurse with a caseload of difficult patients on the night shift might feel she is struggling to come anywhere close to delivering 'Best Possible Care'. During the lengthy and difficult implementation of Agenda for Change, there were many who felt they had 'had less Joy and Pride' than might have been the case. But increasingly, I hear many staff using these terms not with cynicism, but with hope and optimism for the future.

Practising Lean leadership

Whilst leaders have a responsibility to develop visions, they rely on followers to realise them. The most inspiring vision will be empty rhetoric unless anyone wants to put it into action.

The revelation for me since coming to Bolton Hospital has been how using a Lean framework – successful in manufacturing but only very recently applied in hospitals – can transform the way people do their jobs, as well as the service that the patients receive. We call our own adaptation of lean for healthcare 'BICS' – the Bolton Improving Care System.

There are lots of myths about what 'Lean' is and what it isn't. It isn't about being 'Lean and mean', cutting back unthinkingly on the staff available to do a task. Nor is it a recent management fad. It is a systematic approach which has been developed by Toyota over a sixty-year period and which others have adapted in manufacturing and service sectors over the last two decades. Furthermore, Lean isn't something which can be done to you by a management consultancy.

Lean is a way of thinking; a set of principles on which the organisation is founded. At its heart is the ability to think in terms of processes. Patients' journeys through hospitals are long and complex, involving many different individuals and departments – so complex that we rarely, if ever, see the whole journey in its entirety. Instead we manage through a series of silos or boxes labelled: A&E Department, Ward, Theatre. Once we can begin to see the whole of the process, we can see the huge potential for waste, error and delay from the patient's perspective. The job of a Lean Leader is to help others to learn to see this waste and to progressively eliminate it [2].

David Verble is an American engineer. After many years working for US manufacturing organisations, David's career took an unexpected turn. He was appointed by Toyota to promote the Toyota culture across their newly developing US businesses. David has described his sense of culture shock in his first few weeks within Toyota [3].

As an employee in US companies, David was used to elevating problems to his bosses for them to solve. He tried this early on at Toyota, going along to his supervisor to say: 'I am really concerned about this and don't know what to do next'. Rather than being given the answer, he came out with many more questions! The Toyota style of management is based on a fundamental belief that the most motivating thing that you can do is to give people responsibility for solving their own problems. Mr Cho, now Chairman of Toyota and for a time David Verble's boss, has characterised Toyota's approach to Lean Leadership as being: 'go and see; ask why; respect people'.

Go and see

In many NHS Hospitals, the business of management is done in meetings. People who are distant from the job and its problems, called Managers, speculate on the basis of personal anecdotes about what is happening. The solutions proposed are often the result of the latest management fashion, or the whim of the most powerful person in the room. Lean companies take a different approach. They urge Managers to get out of their meeting rooms and 'go to the gemba' which is Japanese for where the work actually happens.

This process of 'go and see' can take place in lots of different ways. Using the formal Lean methodology, multidisciplinary teams of staff are encouraged to map end-to-end patient journeys, deeply understanding the physical processes and information flows involved. This is always surprising and sometimes disconcerting. 'I didn't know we were doing this to patients' is something which clinical staff often say when they map their own processes in detail.

'Go and See' shouldn't simply be restricted to formal Lean improvement activities. It needs to become a habit of mind for all Managers and Clinical Leaders. As soon as a problem arises, the first step should be to go to where the problem is actually happening to talk to staff on the ground and to understand the context of the problem. This has an added side benefit – it makes leadership visible!

In Bolton, we have developed a further version of 'Go and See' which is a hybrid on the patient safety walk arounds which have been pioneered in some organisations. Every week (on a pre-planned rota), an Executive Director visits a Ward, Clinic or Department (including non-clinical areas) and spends up to two hours with the staff and patients. Searching questions are asked in each of the four areas of the Trust's mission. Actions are agreed. Most of these are for the local work area to take forward themselves. Occasionally issues emerge which need to be addressed on a Trust-wide basis. The feedback from these visits is positive and powerful. They are a motivator not only for front line staff but for Directors themselves.

Ask why

In his early experience at Toyota, David Verble was struck most forcibly by the number of questions which Senior Executives asked. What's more, they didn't take a single answer at face value. Lean organisations employ a powerful technique called 'the five whys'. The aim is to continue probing until the root cause of a problem is identified. They also continually ask: What data can help us in solving this problem?

Data are routinely used to help manage a patient's clinical condition (blood pressure, temperature, blood tests, etc.), yet management in Healthcare often feels like a data-free zone. Asking questions and using data are the scientific method applied to management problems.

Respect for people

Going to the workplace to see what is actually happening, and then placing the responsibility on staff to solve their own problems is a demonstration of respect. That respect needs to take other forms too. The use of courteous and moderate language, valuing diversity, showing a genuine interest in the lives of staff outside of work, embodies a deep respect for our work colleagues. A culture of genuine mutual respect and friendliness transmits itself to our patients. It creates a healing environment. Equally, mistrust and a lack of respect reveals itself in poorly co-ordinated services and indifference to patients' needs.

One of the classic tools of the quality improver is the 'Plan–Do–Check–Adjust cycle'. The most under-used part of this cycle is that of 'check'. In many organisations we suffer from repeated cycles of 'plan do–plan do–plan do'. We constantly underestimate the importance of reflection. We will only become more effective leaders if we take the time to learn from our experiences and to adjust the way we work.

Managing yourself

It turns out that becoming a good Manager of other people, starts with learning to manage yourself. I have a feeling that this is a realisation that came to me somewhat late in the day! In the early part of my career, I majored on energy, enthusiasm and a desire to make change happen. I didn't always pause to consider the impact of those changes on others. Nor did I always realise that my enthusiasm to get things done could easily turn into someone else's crushing workload (sadly, this may well still be the case at times).

The reason that this is so important for any leader is that they have a huge impact on those they lead. As Tom Peters has noted, managers have got into a habit of complaining about the fact that they have had power taken away from them, by regulation, Trade Unions, the economic climate or other forces beyond their control. Peters disagrees. He says, 'The Manager is shockingly powerful.' People pay attention to the things that Managers care about and sadly also to what they don't care about [4].

Stephen Covey, in his book *The 7 Habits of Highly Effective People*, gives good advice on how to go about managing yourself better [5]. He explains why this is important if you hope to add value to the relationships you have with others.

The good news is that the requirement to develop self-awareness and better control of your own actions and emotions is highly consistent with practising a lean style of leadership. A lean leader needs the self-confidence to allow others to make mistakes and learn lessons for themselves. On the plus side, you can also receive great coaching insights and feedback from your peers and from those who work for you, if you listen hard enough to the signals.

Perhaps one of the greatest challenges for any leader is getting the right balance between optimism and realism. I know that this is something with which I have struggled in the past. Indeed I have been described as 'a relentless optimist' which I am not altogether sure was a compliment! It is all too easy to let your exuberance and your wish for things to go well, to delude you into thinking things are going better and people are feeling more motivated than is actually the case.

At the same time it's also a risk particularly when you first embark on a lean transformation, that you will become overwhelmed by problems. Once you learn to see waste, it is everywhere. This is especially so in hospitals where waste can imply treatments delayed, patients waiting in pain, errors leading to actual harm and relatives whose memories of the last days of their loved ones are marred by problems that need not have existed.

Keeping your optimism up in such circumstances isn't easy, but it is essential. Jim Collins argues that one of the hallmarks of organisations that make the leap to greatness is that they master what he calls the 'honesty/ faith paradox' [6]. Such organisations are brutally honest with themselves about the facts of their own position. They actively seek out problems and are self critical of their own performance. Typically if things go well, they attribute it to luck or to a favourable external climate. If things are going badly, they are hard on themselves. Yet at the same time these organisations never for a moment lose the belief that some day they will make the transformational leap into delivering excellent performance.

This is a paradox which I have worked hard to try to master myself. Given that I am by nature an optimist, it means learning to surround myself with people who will be realists and point out the flaws in my plans. It also means not becoming too impatient with them when they do this!

This is something we talk about a lot in Bolton and is a central feature of our BICS work. We aim to 'go and see' – to look for and find problems to fix. If we succeed we celebrate; if we don't, we will be back tomorrow, the day after and for as long as it takes until we do get the problem fixed.

I count myself as incredibly lucky to have had such a satisfying and fulfilling career. I have learned much (a lot of it the hard way) and I am sure I have got a great deal more still to learn. I now understand that building an inspiring vision and telling it many times over is not only important for your organisation but also personally rewarding. I can see how Lean as a transformational methodology can open your eyes to a whole world of waste and opportunity for improvement. It can also reveal the massive potential that exists in each and every member of staff. We spend a large part of our waking lives at work, but often use so little of the talents and abilities that are available to us. Finally, I have come to learn that knowing myself what's important and what's not, has to be the starting point for presuming to lead others. Perhaps it's that recently-found level of self-awareness that means I now think of my career much more as a climbing frame, rather than a ladder to ascend. I am looking forward to many more exciting ups and downs and leaps into the unknown in the years ahead.

References

1. Lencioni, P. (2007) *The Three Signs of a Miserable Job*. San Francisco: Jossey-Bass.
2. Fillingham, D. (2008) *Lean Healthcare*. Chichester: Kingsham Press.
3. Verble, D. Unpublished presentation in Sydney, February 2007.
4. Peters, T. (1985) *A Passion for Excellence*. New York: Random House.
5. Covey, S. (1989) *The 7 Habits of Highly Effective People*. Sydney: Simon and Schuster.
6. Collins, J. (2001) *Good To Great*. London: Random House.

8

LEADERSHIP BY AMBITION
Stephen Dalton

I was one of several colleagues who was involved at the outset of the formation of the NHS North West Leadership Academy. I recall being interviewed by a colleague who was involved in developing the brochure for the Academy. She asked me what I thought leadership was all about and I remember talking for some time on the subject. When the brochure came out, I was quoted as saying that 'leadership is about creating a sense of direction and then harnessing the potential of the people around you for the greater good of the enterprise'. Our people are our greatest assets and we do them an injustice if we do not value and make use of their potential. As an extension to this we should also aspire to wanting the best of our people. I have personally come to believe and practise what I call 'leadership by ambition'. For me, this is about the need for leaders to jointly create a vision that can take the organisation to a higher level of functioning; to aim higher than just meeting targets or surviving within budgets; and in sum to foster leadership by ambition. Placing ladders for me is about helping to create a context in which leadership by ambition can be owned and practised at all levels within the organisation.

I want to begin my story by focusing on being on the receiving end of having ladders being placed for me as the experience has had a formative and lasting effect on my leadership role to this day. I joined the NHS as a nurse and on reflection had little or no aspiration beyond a clinical managerial role. But I worked in Merseyside during the 1980s when there was a trend for talent-spotting driven by the then Regional Health Authority. The existing culture was one in which leaders were encouraged to create opportunities for individuals with potential to grow. This was certainly a progressive trend that challenged the 'time serving/experience is good' tradition that was the dominant model of human resource practices.

In a very short space of time, I was promoted from a clinical manager role, to a Director's post, to a Chief Executive in 1995. This career progression has had a lasting impact on my leadership role. It has caused me to think about and value the potential of the people I work with and I have adopted an approach that nurtures talented people who have the confidence and ambition to make things happen within the organisation.

The NHS has many able and talented people and we can achieve more by harnessing such talent. Many capable individuals, particularly in the middle strata of organisation, still have images and experiences of climbing ladders as being very difficult. The mantra that our people are our best assets is only meaningful if we are able to both value and make use of what they bring to the organisation. We need our leaders to help others to step forward, and to provide them with opportunities to stretch by the right kind of nurturing and support. Progressive organisations should in effect have a range of strategies that recognise and nurture talent. Whilst long apprenticeships were the norm and still are the case for many individuals, we should be able to identify and fast track talent development on a case-by-case basis.

In many ways I have had the good fortune of a working with many able and talented people who saw in me some potential that they were prepared to invest in. My own direct experience of this at a very senior level was by the Chairman who appointed me to my first post as Chief Executive. The organisation had just lost its CEO and there was a lot of work to do to turn things around. The Chairman was prepared to take a risk with me and gave me a lot of freedom to create a culture for making things happen and in effect there was a lot to do.

Since those formative years, on more than one occasion in my Chief Executive career, I've walked into failing organisations that lacked ambition and were happy to languish in mediocrity and learned helplessness.

These circumstances require unfaltering determination to not just move from 'weak' to 'fair' but make the step change to excellence. Leadership of this ambition requires courage, energy, skilful management through the application of high quality performance systems which make a difference and, in the case of health services, real clinical engagement.

Turning around weak organisations are not always the most attractive jobs but I've found they are, by far, the most rewarding. There is a need to ignore the doom merchants who will predict the end of your career, certain failure and no chance of attracting talent to support you. On the contrary, the team I have now, who have turned around a failing organisation in what was a failing health economy, are some of the most talented individuals any organisation would be lucky to attract.

Many of my colleagues, not only in the North West but across the country, have had to lead and manage turnaround organisations. Each case would have had their own distinctive issues and agendas and as a consequence their own approaches. My approach consisted of a set of actions including:

- Gaining the confidence of my team and leadership across the whole organisation
- Enthusing them to be ambitious
- Being accessible and walking the floor to listen and to have conversations
- Telling people that they were good, valued and that they were key to our being able to turn around the crisis at our organisation.

Leadership of a failing organisation requires the entire leadership team to be committed and engaged. My role here was to create ladders by giving focus and responsibility to my senior team and to enable them to contribute imaginatively to the tasks at hand. In situations of crisis, one needs to create a vision that can deliver small gains quickly which can provide a motivating impact. But a top team, or for that matter any team, which is disunited will not deliver to their potential. My response when encountering failing organisations was to appeal to senior colleagues to share the ambition or leave. Often they'll leave. It is best in these circumstances that top teams both co-create, share and own the improvement agenda so that energy and effort can be harnessed in the same direction.

The need to replace senior colleagues has afforded me two useful tactics. My walking the flooring and knowing what was happening within the organisation enabled me to identify talent and I was able to promote a number of internal colleagues to senior posts. These were well respected and credible colleagues who were able to carry their teams as well as delivering on objectives agreed. Whilst, in some cases, I recognised that they were relatively inexperienced, I knew that they had potential and could see even early on that they were thriving in their post.

It's not all about internal talent management and it's important to recognise the need to import talent to maintain the pace of change. It is important to also make critical turnkey appointments that can make a step change in quality of leadership and systems management.

With a committed and ambitious team on board, we were able to galvanise energies to a set of key objectives to lead and deliver success. Now, most effort in turnaround is to secure financial stability. But I saw this as an opportunity of going much higher. Financial stability, yes; but how about using the opportunity for improving the quality of care and services, to increase patient and staff satisfaction. This is the moment in the journey when those I referred to earlier as being happy to languish in mediocrity and learned helplessness will do their best to drag you down. Ambition and success can hold up a mirror to others.

Whilst all our original ambitions have been realised, the ambition to move from good to great remains strong, and sometimes elusive. A culture of continuous improvement is the legacy of the journey to date.

The NHS is not only the only the third largest employer in the world, but in the UK context spends over a £110 billion a year. As leaders at all levels in the organisation, we owe it to our patients and our paymasters alike to strive to give of our best in the use of such resources. Our role is to enthuse and support our people to aim high and to give of their best continually. Ambition for me is healthy if it is about the good of the organisation, the patients we serve and the wider community.

We all know that organisations have lifecycles of their own. Johannsen's (2008) work has shown that there are distinctive stages from start-up, to expansion, to stabilisation, to crisis or decline, to dissolution or re-creation. And we know that successful organisations and companies will have to face up to crises or decline at some stage as the review by *Business Week* (1984) has shown in respect of the companies discussed in the classic book by Peters and Waterman (1982), *In Search of Excellence*.

There is now some renewed interest in the role of ambition in organisational life. In their new book, *The Arc of Ambition*, James Champy and Nitin Nohria (2000), have asserted that: *'ambition is the root of all achievement.*

Without ambition, no conquests are made, no lands are discovered and no businesses are created, let alone reengineered.'

They have shown that:

'... the careers of ambitious people typically follow a predictable path – their so-called arc of ambition. The curve of the arc isn't necessarily the same for every individual. For some, the rise of the curve is slow. ... then, as the curve rises, these dreams provide a springboard for action. ... for others, the curve rises quickly. Ambition thrusts them into the limelight, sometimes right onto the world stage, at an amazingly early age.'

The mindset of such individuals is about doing and building something bigger and they can be categorised as one of three types as follows:

- **Creators** – those who are innovators and pioneers
- **Capitalisers** – who were able to exploit technological developments to the market place;
- **Consolidators** – the professional managers in business, the arts etc who are ambitious to make new technologies work consistently and profitably in corporate settings.

Champy and Nohria argue that 'ambition has always required creativity, daring and timing' but in our present context these on their own are not enough; whilst we need perseverance and skill, we also need ambition of exceptional intensity to succeed. They suggested that:

'perhaps the worthiest ambition is the one that goads us to make the best of whatever talents or conditions life hands us. We see no virtue in a gifted person who squanders his or her gifts. We rightly admire even a modestly talented person who strives to surpass all expectations. We expect ambition to pay off in something beneficial and respect ambition that adds value to a business, to a community, to knowledge, to life itself.'

So why an arc of ambition? Their assumption is that it is nothing new and in effect is the creative process that *transforms dreams into reality*. They see ambition as the key to the human condition and as such should be nurtured and encouraged far and wide. Champy and Nohria commented that:

'the human story is fundamentally about people overcoming obstacles and rising triumphantly on the arc of ambition. The story has a cast of millions, in which we all have a part.'

The role of leaders is therefore to create the right set of conditions and environment in which others can thrive and give of their best. We can all contribute to this as outlined by Champy and Nohria by:

- Seeing what others do not;
- Following a steadfast path;
- Seizing the moment;
- Tempering ambition;
- Inspiring with a greater purpose;
- Never violating values;
- Keeping control by not giving up;
- Changing or dying; or
- Leaving gracefully.

References

Business Week (1984) 'Oops. Who's excellent now?' 5 November, pp. 76–88.

Champy, J. & Nohria, N. (2000) *The Arc of Ambition: Defining the Leadership Journey.* Cambridge, MA: Perseus.

Johannsen, M. (2008) Five phases of the organisation life cycle. http://www.legacee.com/FastGrowth/OrgLifeCycle.html

Peters, T. & Waterman, R. (1982) *In Search of Excellence.* San Francisco: Harper & Row.

9

VALUE-DRIVEN LEADERSHIP

James Birrell

'Values are the essence of who we are as human beings. Our values get us out of bed every morning, help us select the work we do, the company we keep, the relationship we build and ultimately the groups and organisations we lead. Our values influence every decision and move we make, even to the point of how we choose to make our decisions.'

Rue (2001)

Introduction

The literature on leadership is voluminous and as a result one may have expected to find a definitive answer as to what constitutes effective leadership. The problem in part lies in the fact that there are as many views and perspectives as there are writers, theorists and commentators. It is perhaps nearer the truth to suggest that there are a myriad of ways in which leadership can be described, demonstrated and understood. The very wide array of accounts can be very confusing for those taking early steps on the ladder towards achieving the various goals they have set for themselves.

In my view, an individual's leadership skills, behaviour and insights develop over time based upon their experience, knowledge and exposure to approaches adopted by others through role modelling, experiential learning and, yes, practice. This particular chapter will not set out to define precisely how leadership can or should be provided. Instead I would like to share our experience at Aintree as to how we have developed a value-driven leadership framework by constructing a template within which managers can function in a consistent and cohesive manner at bringing a sense of order and clarity to their leadership role.

Leadership styles and qualities

In my own experience, I have observed and have been part of leadership practices and approaches that can be provided in many different ways. Amongst the different types of approaches are the following:

- *Autocratic approach* – what I say goes
- *Democratic approach* – the majority view will prevail
- *Leadership by decibel* – whoever speaks loudest will determine the outcome
- *Leadership by default* – where a vacuum exists, leadership decisions are often reached by default
- *Charismatic leadership* – people will (up to a point) follow what a charismatic leader says regardless of the content
- *Leadership by collective agreement* – all sign up to a specific course of action
- *Leadership by diktat* – an order is issued which has to be followed by all.

Equally leaders can have many different qualities, and to illustrate that you just need to look at some famous and infamous leaders of the past and present, e.g. Napoleon, Adolf Hitler, Winston Churchill, Margaret Thatcher, George Bush and Robert Mugabe. Amongst the qualities they have displayed have been the following (note: these are not mutually exclusive):

- Intelligence
- Wisdom
- Experience
- Vision
- Luck
- Contacts/networking ability
- Unreasonableness
- Fear and manipulation
- Courage
- Determination

The purpose of listing these approaches and qualities is simply to show that there is no single recipe for constructing a leader. There is a lot of truth in the statement 'Cometh the Hour, Cometh the Man' because very often the leaders that emerge in given situations/circumstances probably would not have risen to the top at other times. Winston Churchill is almost certainly a case in point here. Prior to the Second World War, it looked very much like his time had passed, yet when the need for a strong, focussed leader arose, Winston Churchill emerged and subsequently became one of the greatest leaders of all time.

Following on from the above point, it is clearly important to take into account the circumstances surrounding a role when deciding upon both the style of leadership required and the skills needed to fulfil the task. The approach differs according to seniority, specific responsibilities, numbers of staff managed, etc. There can also be a difference between the ways in which leadership is provided in different types of business or sectors. In the public sector, for example, there are clear standards of behaviour to be adopted which take into account the need for public accountability plus explicit public sector values. The NHS adds into this mix the concepts of service provision and the drive to provide quality services rather than pursue profit or personal gain.

Organisational values

An organisation ideally should have sustainability, consistency and provide valuable and valued services. Achieving this requires far more than a one-dimensional approach to leadership. There needs to be an underpinning system of values and behaviours which can be linked through to an organisation's vision and objectives.

Accepting the premise that it is important to establish an organisation's values in order to shape the ways in which leadership is provided, it is clearly important to understand the culture, maturity and ambitions of the organisation which is to be led. For example, Aintree University Hospitals NHS Foundation Trust is recognised as a friendly, hard working organisation with a significant proportion of the workforce living close to the hospital. It is not hierarchical by nature, is used to working as a large team rather than individual discrete areas, and takes pride in providing quality services. This description begins to set natural parameters and indicators for the values to be adopted.

It is also important to understand and take into account the personal qualities and approach of the key leaders/managers within the organisation. There is little point in adopting a set of values and behaviours if people subsequently cannot or will not align with them. There is so much merit in adopting a whole system approach – at developing and co-creating the set of values that are important for the organisation. Many of us will know of the set of values developed by Don Berwick of the Institute of Healthcare Improvement [IHI] and modified slightly by the then Modernisation Agency of the NHS as:

- no needless death or disease;
- no needless pain;
- no feelings of helplessness (amongst service users and staff);
- no unwanted delay;
- no waste; and
- no inequality in service delivery.

Whatever set of values have been identified and worked through to develop this process, the proposed values should be discussed within the organisation to ensure that there will be broad buy-in, launched widely and lived by leaders at all levels.

Adopting values will help to establish a way of working. This can then be combined with national and local drivers and demands to develop organisational objectives and a vision for the organisation which is reflective of the Trust's aspirations.

In the case of Aintree, the values we have signed up to are as follows:

- **Quality and safety**
- **Compassion, dignity and respect**
- **Openness, honesty and consistency**
- **Two-way communication**
- **Learn from mistakes**
- **Individual accountability**

When these values are coupled with various must-dos and the organisation's desire to provide safe, high quality patient care, it came as little surprise to staff when the vision adopted by the Trust was 'to provide high quality patient-centred healthcare and proactively enhance the Trust's local, national and international reputation.'

On a day-to-day basis, the values and vision now provide a backdrop against which decisions are taken. This includes matters of strategic as well as operational importance. This approach/philosophy needs to be adopted across the organisation and not just at the most senior levels. For this to happen, staff need to have confidence that their leaders and managers will 'walk the walk' as well as 'talk the talk'. Ensuring that this happens is in itself a key leadership task.

Whilst values, the associated behaviours and the overall vision have to be sacrosanct and applied consistently, this does not mean that they cannot evolve or develop over time. For example, increasingly over the last 18 months, the emphasis on profitability and productivity has been replaced by a very strong focus on quality, patient safety and improving the patient experience. Similarly, compassion now sits alongside dignity and respect. These are all logical extensions to the existing values and as such will require little dialogue with staff prior to adoption.

Shaping leadership through application of values

So much for theory, but how does it apply in practice? The following case studies illustrate how value-driven leadership has worked at Aintree which will hopefully serve to illustrate how the values have helped to shape the ways in which managers discharge their leadership responsibilities.

EXAMPLE 1

NHS Trusts have always been aware of the importance of good infection control processes and procedures. However, their importance has grown significantly over recent years to the extent that failure to comply with guidelines is now regarded as a serious matter. Within Aintree we have always ensured that staff are fully trained in all aspects of infection control and have undertaken root cause analyses of instances involving patients catching significant infections. However, the outcome was generally along the lines that there were lessons to be learned and we needed to put more training in place. Rarely were individuals singled out for direct criticism, let alone disciplined. With the raised focus on the subject, we reviewed whether this softly-softly approach was appropriate. This exercise involved assessing alternative action against our values. This resulted in us taking into account the following guiding principles:

- Quality and safety
- Compassion, dignity and respect
- Learn from mistakes
- Individual accountability.

Furthermore, the Trust's vision stressed the importance of 'high quality, patient-centred healthcare'. We concluded that this meant that patient safety had to be at the forefront of our thinking, so a policy of zero tolerance was introduced for failure to comply with infection control guidelines. This means that any breach of the rules results in the relevant staff member being at the very least counselled and possibly taken down the professional misconduct line. This is a fairly dramatic development but because the approach can be clearly linked to the Trust's widely disseminated values and vision, the organisation has accepted that this requires firm and explicit management.

EXAMPLE 2

Another good example of applying the values in practice occurred a few years ago when we had the opportunity to bid to become an Agenda for Change pilot site. Within the Trust, particularly within the HR department, there was a realisation of how much work would be involved if we were chosen to participate. However, we took the view that Agenda for Change would represent a significant shift/improvement in how pay within the NHS was determined, which was very much in accordance with our principles of consistency, dignity and respect. The decision was therefore taken to apply and the Trust was successful. The subsequent work did prove to be very onerous but many of our staff received significant pay rises a year before Agenda for Change was formally rolled out to the rest of the NHS. As a consequence, the Board's decision was greatly appreciated throughout the organisation which reinforced the importance of values and helped to generate faith and confidence in the Trust's leadership and valuing of our people.

EXAMPLE 3

In some organisations it can be difficult to comply with the 'openness' value. However, partly because Aintree adopted it as a key value, it is now second nature for managers to convey to staff exactly what is going on around issues such as performance, financial position, developments, staffing matters, etc. The only things that tend not to be revealed are matters of a personal nature or areas of commercial confidence and even then an explanation is made for why the information cannot be revealed. This has had the dual benefits of minimising the number of unhealthy rumours which circulate whilst giving staff the confidence to ask questions of their manager in the knowledge that they will get an honest answer. The process is not always about conveying good news. Openness also means that we tell the organisation as soon as possible of issues such as cost improvement programme targets, the need for productivity gains, problems around infection control, the contents of patients' complaint letters, etc. The net impact is that staff feel involved in decisions, which in many studies has been shown to produce a more motivated workforce.

EXAMPLE 4

One of the beneficial impacts of the existence of values is that staff are very aware of how they should behave towards each other. Whilst there is still the occasional fall out, sometimes in a spectacular fashion, there is a general awareness and acceptance that everybody has to be treated with dignity and respect, regardless of role or grade. This has proved pivotal in some disciplinary matters, particularly in the early stages when decisions are being taken about the handling of a potentially serious matter. It has also prevented a blind eye being turned towards more senior staff. It is much easier to withstand pressures that are brought to bear such as 'shroud-waving' or the presence of 'old boy networks' when something is clearly contrary to an established value. The effect of this has been that there are far fewer incidents of bullying or harassment plus staff are confident that everybody is treated the same, regardless of grade or seniority.

EXAMPLE 5

Treating people with dignity and respect can mean different things to different people so we have tried to clarify our expectations. This culminated in a local initiative which we called 'Valuing People'. It involves staff undergoing what to all intents and purposes is a customer care strategy but with no differentiation between patients, visitors or colleagues. The programme highlights 6 factors that underpin the Aintree approach to customer care, i.e.

- **Listen**
- **Communicate**
- **Be polite**
- **Smile**
- **Work as a team**
- **Be respectful.**

The approach has had a reasonable degree of success, particularly in terms of ensuring that staff have a good awareness of the behaviours expected of them when dealing with people on behalf of the Trust. A further initiative emerged from the focus on dignity and respect – the introduction of '**You said, we did**' boards. This is a scheme shamelessly copied from elsewhere which enables us to demonstrate to patients how we are acting upon the issues they raise. The approach has been greeted enthusiastically by the Patients Council and the Board of Governors as they can see clear evidence of the Trust's willingness to address problems. Both the 'Valuing People' initiative and the 'You said, we did' boards are examples of visible leadership which have arisen from the values adopted by the organisation.

Our experience to date has been one that has provided much learning and cultural change. As leaders, we can derive considerable understanding from making time to discover our set of values that are balanced and healthy. They enable us to act with integrity and for the good of our organisation, people and patients. They are powerful at enabling us and others to understand why we make the decisions we have made. They enable us to enable others to aspire to higher performance.

Conclusions

Leadership can be provided in many ways and there is no single blueprint that should be followed by aspirant leaders. Styles and qualities are shaped more by experience than the contents of management textbooks. However, defining, shaping and applying leadership becomes a more straightforward task when it is done against an agreed set of values and behaviours. These provide a context within which decisions can be taken which helps an organisation to establish a consistent direction and the staff to have confidence and belief in management. Whilst this does not necessarily guarantee success due to the wide range of external and uncontrollable influences, it should produce a more contented workforce which will result in higher productivity.

References

Rue, B. (2001) Values-based leadership. *Programme Manager*, July–August, pp. 12–15.

10

CHAMPIONING INTEGRATION AND PARTNERSHIP WORKING IN KNOWSLEY

Anita Marsland, MBE

P lacing Ladders within an organisation that connects top, middle and front line is beneficial in more ways than one, as we have seen earlier. With Local Government and NHS responsibilities increasingly overlapping in the areas of Public Health and Social Care, integrated working is becoming more important. Placing ladders is arguably also about strategic alliances and partnerships with organisations that operate outside the NHS. In this chapter I want to share some of the learning and insights that we have garnered through the championing of integration and partnership working in Knowsley. The story will detail the pioneering approach adopted by Knowsley Metropolitan Borough Council and NHS Knowsley (the PCT for the borough), of which I am the Chief Executive. I am also Executive Director of Wellbeing Services (incorporating social care, leisure and cultural services). In effect I am a joint appointment between the PCT and the Council.

My early career in social work began with Liverpool Social Services where, having gained a professional social work qualification at Liverpool University, I continued to work in various roles as Practitioner and Manager for a period of 19 years. I moved to Wigan MBC in 1993, where I held appointments as Assistant Director Children and Families and Deputy Director of Social Services. I was then appointed as Director of Knowsley Social Services in 2000, later being appointed to the joint post when the PCT was established in April 2002.

As Lead Director for Children's Services for ADSS North West, I have been involved in providing strategic leadership for a range of regional developments including Quality Projects and latterly the establishment of the North West Regional Strategic Partnership for Children and Young People, of which I am a Vice Chair. I am also a Member of Health England National Reference Group for Health and Wellbeing which reports to the Secretary of State for Health. I was recently appointed to the LGA Health Commission and received an MBE in the Queen's New Year's Honours List 2008, for services to Health and Social Care.

I describe myself as, first and foremost, a public servant and I am passionate about improving people's lives in Knowsley which is the shared objective of the PCT and the Council.

Knowsley has a population, with significant social, economic and health needs. Life expectancy for both males and females is significantly below that in England. For males, it can vary by as much as ten years from parts of Stockbridge Village to Halewood, with similar differences seen in female life expectancy. Such variances are unacceptable to both NHS Knowsley and the Council alike and we are determined to reduce these inequalities. Health needs across the Borough are dominated by cardiovascular disease, cancer and respiratory disease, with mortality levels significantly higher than those in England and Wales.

From the very beginning of the partnership between the Council and the PCT, a decision was made to place the needs of Knowsley residents at the forefront of public service and that, together, health and social services could make a real and sustainable difference to improving the lives of those who live in the Borough. My joint appointment marked a new beginning for both organisations.

The role of the leader as has been discussed elsewhere in the publication includes setting direction, selling a vision, strengthening alignment and harnessing effort and capability to deliver a quality service. But it sometimes requires the taking of calculated and, on occasion, personal risk. My accepting the joint appointment was one such case as HR practice in 2002 was underdeveloped to legislate for such a unique appointment. But I regarded this risk as secondary to the benefits of having an integrated leadership position and the opportunities that that would lead to join up strategies and policies to improve lives in the borough. I have relished the opportunities integrated working brings and have been able to establish a wonderful integrated Leadership Team that has become expert in 'managing ambiguity'.

A formal partnership under what is now Section 75 of the Health Act was quickly established which I feel 'provides a single accountability with dual governance. Our common purpose is to serve the people of Knowsley'.

Earlier this year, the Council decided to restructure its directorates and I grasped the opportunity to bring Leisure and Cultural Services together with Social Services, into a new Directorate of 'Wellbeing Services'. Through this, the partnership between the Council and PCT has been strengthened and we now refer to ourselves as Knowsley 'Health & Wellbeing'. Our commissioning responsibilities now extend beyond health and social care, into such activities as sports and leisure centres, community services, arts and culture. These new services bring further opportunities for us to develop initiatives impacting upon lifestyle, personal behaviour and responsibility.

Far from being a collision of cultures, partnership working has ensured the efficiency and effectiveness of services provided by integrated and co-located teams by providing one point of contact for service users. At an organisational level, my health and local authority responsibilities are discharged with the help of a single unified Executive Leadership Team or ELT. This provides a strong and effective executive, cutting through administrative boundaries and structures and has resulted in aligning individual skills and competencies to local need. Work is typically managed in a matrix manner, with an executive lead identified for all key business objectives and tasks, pulling together talent from across directorates to deliver the objective in hand.

I am often asked about barriers and conflicts of interest in respect of integrated and partnership working and my retort is that in my own context they do not exist – 'only opportunities'. A concrete example of the maturity of the partnership is the range of pooled budgets which we manage to best effect, recognising the pressures across our organisations.

Being the 'blue smartie' is what I liken the working arrangements in Knowsley to! Sometimes 'our approach is in the spotlight and other times it is not, but I do highly recommend it in terms of improving performance'. The Commission for Social Care Inspection has, for 3 years, rated Knowsley's Social Services as a 3 star organisation which includes the judgements of 'excellent' for services, and 'excellent' for capacity to improve while the latest Health Care Commission rated NHS Knowsley with an overall rating of excellent, one of only 9 PCTs in the country to achieve this very high standard and demonstrating significant improvements over the past 2 years.

Our achievements have been made possible by the able and committed people who work within the range of professionals across the PCT and the Council and I have masses of respect for these colleagues who make a difference to people's lives every day and who have all contributed to these consistently improving results.

Our organisation, like others, was recently heavily involved in the World Class Commissioning assessment process. I have reflected on the learning and insights derived from the health and wellbeing commissioning arrangements which we feel have benefited greatly from the experience of Social Care commissioning since the 1990s.

Our commissioning arrangements are organised with executive leads for the five key areas of:

- secondary care/hospital services;
- prevention and wellbeing;
- integrated community services;
- primary care; and
- urgent care.

Responsibility for children is led by the local authority Director of Children's Services, who delegates the delivery of health and social care services to me. Critical to the effective commissioning of services to meet local need is the engagement and involvement of our partners in the three local Practice-based Commissioning Consortia, alongside the clinical input from our colleagues in the Professional Executive Committee. We have been striving to be a World Class Commissioner 'not as an end in itself but because World Class Commissioning will bring about the truly personalised services that people deserve'.

In taking this forward what are the lessons and insights from which we can learn?

1. Firstly, it is obvious, as mentioned at the outset, that effective leadership of integrated and joint working requires a great deal of goodwill and commitment at all levels. Each partnering organisation will need to be explicit at the outset as to their shared values and strategic objectives.

2. To make integrated working sustainable, a clear and simple operating framework, such as our Section 75 Partnership Agreement, provides for single accountability with dual governance.

3. The need for an integrated communication strategy is paramount. This includes ensuring key messages are communicated across the organisation in a systematic way but also taking time to personally deliver these messages and allow colleagues the opportunity to network informally. We have twice-yearly staff communication events at venues across the borough and, together with our NHS Knowsley Chair and Directorate Portfolio Holder, I am able to share strategic objectives and thank staff for going the extra mile.

4. Perhaps the single most important factor is that of bringing on board all our people from grass roots upwards. Leadership at the varying levels of our organisations are empowered to test and get on with things. It is here where we can nurture creativity that can deliver on service improvement. We value and promote bottom-up integration. This is where the real difference is experienced and this is where we are able to move closer to our ambition of Improving People's Lives in Knowsley.

11

CO-CREATING EFFECTIVE PARTNERSHIP AND TEAMWORK

Sheena Cumiskey

I was at the start of the inception of the NHS NW Leadership Academy. I strongly subscribed to the view, shared by many of my colleagues, that our own development was crucial towards world class standards and excellence in care provision in our community. At the very outset, we had made a major commitment to develop and sustain leadership potential as we felt that it was through nurturing and sustaining talent that we could help to make a difference at service improvement that could impact upon the lives of our patients and our staff alike. I am delighted that the Academy's varied set of development programmes are impacting on our community of leaders. I therefore welcome the opportunity to share insights and experience of our learning as a means of engaging and involving our community to sustain service improvement at all levels in our organisations.

My own story about placing ladders will focus on co-creating effective teamwork. It represents, for me, a simple yet effective whole system engagement of placing ladders. But it is also a manifestation of the energy and effort that can be collectively harnessed within an organisation to deliver quality patient care. Furthermore, the story also symbolises the valuable experience and learning that I have derived from a ladder that was placed for me by the Chair of the organisation of my last appointment. This is a story of learning derived from staff partnership working based on my experiences as a CEO post at a large District General Hospital. The vision for this came from an idea set off with the Chair who appointed me to the Trust and of our vision to provide effective patient care by working in partnership with staff.

The role of leaders in driving service transformation and change is paramount in terms of **setting direction**. Here, the emphasis as outlined in the Leadership Quality Framework document is about setting:

'a vision for the future, drawing on their political awareness of the health and social care context. This political astuteness and their vision for the future is underpinned by Intellectual flexibility, coupled with Drive for results. This sense of Seizing the future is key in inspiring and motivating others to work with them.'

It is useful to refresh our minds about the distinctive aspects and features of the setting direction dimension and their inclusion here is to emphasise their importance of the role of boards at looking at the big picture as follows:

Seizing the future
High performing leaders ACT NOW to shape the future. They are motivated to take action to achieve a radically different future – one in which health services are truly integrated and focused on the needs of patients.

Features of this quality include:
- Making the most of current opportunities to bring about improvements that are of benefit to staff, carers or patients.
- Being able to interpret the likely direction of changes in the health service and beyond – using their political astuteness.
- Using their insights into the broad strategic direction of health and social care to help shape and implement the approaches and culture in their organisation, and to influence developments across the wider health and social care context.
- Underpinning their vision and action with a strong focus on local needs.
- Being prepared to undertake transformational, rather than just incremental, change where this will achieve service improvement.

Intellectual flexibility
High performing leaders are quickly able to assess a situation and to draw pragmatic conclusions. They are able to switch between the significant detail and the big picture to shape a vision – for their own service, organisation or across the wider health context.

Features of this quality include:

- Being receptive to fresh insights and perspectives from diverse sources, both internal and external to the organisation (driven by their values of inclusiveness and service improvement).
- Understanding that change may have to be radical to achieve health improvement.
- Being open to innovative thinking and encouraging creativity and experimentation in others too.

Broad scanning

High performing leaders in the health service demonstrate high levels of seeking and networking for information. By keeping abreast of developments, both locally and nationally, they are best positioned to shape the vision for a service or organisation as well as understand how to influence others.

Features of this quality include:

- Making it a priority to know about how services are being delivered and what the experience is of patients and users on the ground.
- Being persistent in getting the key facts of a situation.
- Having systematic ways of informing themselves about key developments.

Political astuteness

Outstanding leaders demonstrate a political astuteness about what can and cannot be done in how they set targets and identify service improvements.

Features of this quality include:

- Understanding the climate and culture in their own organisation and in the wider health and social care environment.
- Knowing who the key influencers are – both internally and externally to the organisation – and how to go about involving them, as required.
- Being attuned to health strategy and policy at a national and local level and being able to plan a way ahead that takes account of these strategies.
- Understanding that the role of leader in the health service is now broader than simply being responsible for one organisation and that no one organisation in the health service can be 'stand alone'.

Drive for results

High performing leaders are motivated to transform the services for patients and thereby to improve quality. The personal qualities at the core of the framework provide the energy and the sheer determination which fuel Drive for results.

Features of this quality include:

- Setting ambitious targets which may exceed the minimum standard required and taking calculated risks – all with the aim of delivering added value to the service.
- Focusing their own, and others', energy on what really makes a difference, rather than being constrained by methods which were used in the past.
- Actively seeking out opportunities to improve delivery of service through partnership and new ways

www.NHSLeadershipQualities.nhs.uk

Facets of these functions were uppermost at the setting of our direction of fully engaging the staff within the organisation to deliver on the core objectives and formed the basis of the strategy and framework we developed to enable effective partnership and team working. These ideas are not new and indeed partnership working is now becoming commonplace across the NHS and other organisations. The crucial difference to make it work effectively is having strong commitment at the top.

At the outset we created an overarching set of principles that led us to drive the improvement of patient care. This premise is based on the fact that humans are basically gregarious and work best in teams. Furthermore, we strongly believed that people give of their best to patient care when they feel valued and in control of their environment. It is important that, as leaders, we recognise this and work in partnership with staff to co-create effective patient care and service development.

Mann (2007), based on his experiences of public and private sector partnering, has proposed a number of steps for establishing effective partnerships, six of which are listed here:

1. To be open and explicit about the objectives one is trying to achieve and to encourage partners to be open about theirs both in the short and long term;

2. Be clear – with your partners and your people – about where the boundaries of responsibility lie, not just for the tangible delivery. Who is responsible for the public reputation of the partnership and where will decisions be made that have an impact on it?

3. Be challenging about your own business processes. If the traditional ways you work cause your partner pain then what will that cost you in the long run?

4. Look hard at yourself – are you supporting your partner in words and actions? Staff need a role model of leadership of the partnership – and that starts at the top and should run through all layers of the organisation.

5. Work through a dispute resolution process in advance, so that all parties understand what mediation steps can be invoked, by whom and when.

6. Spend as much personal effort communicating with your partner as you do with your own staff – and expect your partner to do likewise. [To paraphrase a well known politician, it is about communication, communication, communication.]

The NHS has a great many able people who are, day in day out, delivering an effective service. Carrying out a vision for service improvement whist delivering day-to-day services requires a great deal of goodwill, engagement and a commitment to making things happen. A key component to make this real is a champion within the organisation. For us this was our amazing staff-side Chair. She worked as the co-producer in achieving staff partnership throughout the organisation.

Our focus was to create the conditions and environment in which people felt valued and able to influence what they are doing and therefore give of their best. We recognised that to create these conditions there needs to be effective trust on both sides, to provide the basis for engaging others. This level of trust can only happen through very effective communication that is open and transparent which operates on the basis of no known secrets on both sides.

Our experience of partnership working made us realise that when people feel that there is an open book approach which is very transparent and that the main focus of the framework is about improving patient care, they are more inclined to give of their best. This is the kernel of it all. Again these ideas are not new. They have been explicitly spelt out in the Leadership Qualities Framework in respect of Delivering Service Improvement as follows:

Leading change through people
Outstanding leaders are focused on articulating the vision with compelling clarity, keeping the focus on change and inspiring others to be positive in their support of service improvement.

Features of this quality include:
- Gaining the support of others by ensuring that they understand the reasons behind the change.
- Sharing leadership – with the team and others in the organisation and in partner organisations.
- Encouraging others, especially front line staff, to find new ways of delivering and developing services and to take the lead in implementation of change.
- Demonstrating a highly visible, authoritative and democratic leadership style which is underpinned by strongly held values around equality, diversity and openness.
- Taking a collaborative or facilitative approach in working in partnership with diverse groups.
- Enabling teams, within the organisation and across the health community, to work effectively together, helping to unblock obstacles, identifying and securing resources, and taking care of teams and of the individuals within them.

www.NHSLeadershipQualities.nhs.uk

Having created the environment, there are then required some mechanisms to make it work. One of the key mechanisms identified early on was the establishment of a staff partnership forum. This allowed staff and managers to meet on an equal footing. The forum was co-chaired by staff-side and management and was the engine house for the whole initiative.

The credibility and effectiveness of the initiative was further enhanced by the staff-side Chair sitting at board level. To make that happen required an enormous degree of trust, not only from board members, but also from the staff-side Chair. Clearly there were issues at board level that members had to feel that the staff-side Chair could handle and deal with in confidence, and that she was also comfortable that she would be heard, and that her voice would be meaningful around the table. In practice this worked really well, which enabled there to be clear and visible leadership from the staff side in taking forward the vision and plans of the board and the opportunity to shape and implement strategies for improvement.

As a practical account to the way we led this, working on an open basis sometimes meant meeting every week and normally every two weeks to share everything that was planned, which included an explicit account of any changes being considered right at the beginning, so that there was an opportunity to shape change before it happened. As is the case in organisational life, we did not always agree about everything; it wasn't always positive but we always came out of it knowing where we were going and how we were going to move things forward and to help shape things back in the engine house of the staff partnership forum. Between meetings time was made for access and communication so that we could tackle issues as they arose.

The staff partnership forum not only operated at a senior, strategic level but right through the organisation so staff-side representatives had a place at the table at each layer of the organisation where teams came together to move things forward or take decisions. This was to ensure that the structure, lines of communication, decision making and action were embedded throughout. The front-line teams that provided direct patient care had the opportunity to be involved there if they so wished. In some parts of the organisation it was more viable and necessary. What is important here is that in each part of the organisation the partnership structures were effective, to enable communication and engagement with their colleagues.

A CEO colleague shared a story about his relationship with senior colleagues on his appointment. A delegation from a clinical directorate required his urgent attention to resolve a clinical matter. At the hastily convened meeting that took place in the actual setting of the problem, he listened carefully and sympathetically and then said to them, 'So what is your solution and how can we achieve it as quickly and as effectively as possible?' The delegation was stunned as they were so used to being told what to do, senior though they are. So they discussed and planned and took action and resolved the matter. In most local situations, people at the source of most problems also have ideas about what will work to solve those problems.

Our work as leaders is about creating the right conditions for the clinical teams to come up with workable solutions. Clear and visible leadership is required at all levels in our organisations and as leaders we need to know when to trust others to make their own decisions. Creating effective partnership at all levels within an organisation also means developing a culture in which colleagues are enabled to co-create a shared vision through active and meaningful engagement where they are trusted as responsible and accountable.

So what difference did this deep engagement of partnership working actually make? A number of tangible results can be singled out and the first of these relates to the impact of this partnership work at helping us to achieve a **3 Stars** rating in performance terms for the organisation not as a one-off but for several years on the run. This acted as a testament to the ability of the organisation to improve performance which made the staff feel far more satisfied in their daily work. It is clear that this would not have been achieved without real buy-in by staff across the organisation. It should be recognised that these kinds of outcomes don't just happen. It requires both a vision, commitment and a mechanism for making it happen. The staff partnership approach enabled the staff to own the targets, particularly by creating a mechanism for the staff to translate the targets into quality improvements for patients and improved working arrangements for the staff.

Another example of the service improvement achieved as a result of the approach was that of the closure of a whole hospital site and relocation of the services to the main hospital site. The staff-side were involved right from the twinkle in the eye of this huge change programme so that they were able to constructively input their ideas for the planning of the move, including what the building would look like, how the services would be delivered and what the implications were for staff. Perhaps most critical of all was their input about the new ways in which they would have to work, including the potential reduction of staff numbers. Due to their input the change went very smoothly without having to resort to compulsory redundancies. This was another major benefit to the effectiveness of the staff partnership. The transfer went so smoothly that within a day of the new building opening, the staff looked as if they had been working there all their lives. Equally heartening was the very positive feedback from patients about their excellent patient experience.

So often changes in health care services don't go smoothly with difficulties of getting effective working once the changes have happened. Our experience points to the kind of evidence one needs to demonstrate as to how effective partnership works. Our insight is that effective partnership brings about effective team work. Belbin's (1993) work has made evident the value of the varied roles that team members bring to the task or work at hand. The evidence from West *et al.* (1999) and Borrill *et al.* (2001) is that team working can make a significant difference in outcomes of quality in health and primary care organisations.

Valuing people

Above all else we were able to make people feel that they were doing valuable work and that they were highly valued in doing this. Crucially, it was also important to ensure that the success achieved during the first year of the 3 Stars rating was not a one-off. By being valued for the work that they were doing, our people feel committed and able to carry service improvement on year on year. The NHS as a public service body cannot exercise the same kinds of reward schemes as practised elsewhere but even within these constraints it was possible and to explore with the staff side what the staff would appreciate. It was agreed that by both the staff-side and by the board that a one-day holiday would be granted as an acknowledgement of the hard work of all staff to achieve their excellent performance. This perception was reinforced by the staff-side survey findings.

So what have we learnt and what are the transferable insights? Well, there are many, but key amongst them is that:

- Leadership is paramount for effective partnerships and teamwork and that this has to be obvious and effective at all levels of the organisation;
- Partners and teams members will handle and act upon sensitive, and at times difficult, information if they trust each other;
- Teams need to have explicit objectives and be clear about each other's roles and responsibilities;
- Communication, shared understanding and clear lines of authority and accountability are vital; and
- Valuing people for the work they do enhances engagement and greater commitment.

References

Belbin, M. (1993) *Team Roles at Work*. London: Butterworth Heinemann.

Borrill, C. *et al.* (2001) The Effectiveness of Health Care Teams in the National Health Service. Report by Universities of Aston, Glasgow, Edinburgh Leeds and Sheffield. Available at: http://homepages.inf.ed.ac.uk/jeanc/DOH-final-report.pdf

Mann, G. (2006) Leadership across a network of alliance. CSIP conference presentation. Available at: http://networks.csip.org.uk/Events/ArchivedEvents/ArchivedEventDetails/?eventID=38

NHSIII: Leadership Qualities Framework. www.NHSleadershipQualities.nhs.uk

West, M. *et al.* (1999) Communication and teamwork in healthcare. *Nursing Times Research*, Vol. 4, No. 1, pp. 8–17.

12

ON BUILDING ALIGNMENT

Derek Campbell

'You can't build a corporation that is fit for the future unless you build a corporation that is fit for human beings... if you can build a company that is fit for its people, that gets the best out of them, you will be a management innovator, you will be a company that can thrive in the world ahead.'

Gary Hamel (2007)

The stories in this publication have focused on the the work of leaders and leadership on the one hand and on the other, some of the key attributes, styles and approaches of leaders. My own story will focus on the work that we have been doing here in Liverpool to ensure that our organisation is best placed to meet the needs of the people we serve through strong alignment with other partnering organisations in the city. Each leadership story in this book also shares something about the leader, their experiences, values, beliefs and motivation. And so I would like to share something of my own background too.

I started my career as a graduate trainee in the Civil Service in 1976. The recruitment officer tried to put me off applying, attaching a note to the information pack saying he had 150 people to see for 30 places and those with good relevant degrees would be favoured. I had a poor non-relevant degree but applied anyway. I got an interview but was turned down. A few days later a letter came informing me that the number of places were increased to 35 and that I was offered place after all. I talked my way into that job. The recruitment manager saw something in me and took a chance; he placed the first ladder and I did not let him down. As I look over my career I can see a number of people who also looked deeper and saw potential and opened doors. In my experience you have to seize that moment and walk through that door.

I entered the NHS in 1989 to a senior finance post. It was a steep learning curve for me and I was fortunate to be working in this setting with a dynamic and well respected Chief Executive. But that Chief Executive left at short notice after only a few months of me being in post. I had no right to expect promotion after such a short time, but spotted an opening and plucked up the courage to have a word. This former CEO contacted the Health Authority in question and I was interviewed and appointed to Director of Finance after only eight months in the NHS. That CEO opened the door, I did the rest.

Later in 1993, I came to Liverpool Health Authority as Director of Finance. Truth is I was going through a sticky patch in my career which can happen when personalities change in a team. Again, doors were opened for me and the rest, as they say, is history, for here I sit fifteen years later in the most marvellous of jobs, Chief Executive of Liverpool PCT.

But let's go back a bit.

In 2002 when the PCTs in Liverpool came into being, I was appointed Chief Executive of Central Liverpool PCT. It was not a natural choice to appoint the outgoing Finance Director of the Health Authority for this post but again, the appointment panel saw something different in me. The Health Economy in Liverpool was in a very poor state after years of decline. I don't think that it is overstating matters to say that the hospitals were working on the edge of system failure on a daily basis after years of capacity reduction with no matching innovation and system change to alleviate pressures. I hope my remarks do not offend anyone. Elaborate and unaffordable capital rebuild schemes were being worked up by providers. Partnership working with the Local Authority was articulated but lacked real substance. In the early years matters were made worse by the creation of three PCTs in the City with inevitable rivalries. We were one of five PCTs in what we described as North Mersey. Work was underway on a clinically-led Model of care which all parties – acute, primary care, local government, clinical and non-clinical, signed up to. But lack of collective leadership caused the model to sit on the shelf after publication.

This was an exciting time to test out ideas but also to deliver early wins. And through some of the work that we were doing I got noticed and was invited to be involved in some national initiatives. For instance I chaired one of the policy taskforce groups on the 'Our Health, Our Care, Our Say' white paper (the only NHS manager to do so) and later was invited onto the Advisory Board to Ministers (again, the only NHS manager to be on the group). I remain keen to maximise the learning that such involvement affords and encourage colleagues to participate whenever such opportunities arise.

I concentrated on forging ahead in Central Liverpool. We published a comprehensive strategy by the end of 2002 and we took risks in developing capacity in that first year with major recruitment of nurses and GPs into the system. Personally I concentrated in developing my relationship, and standing, with the acute sector and the City council as well as going the extra mile to win the support of primary care. Over the next few years it was about building credibility with those players, both in myself and my organisation, to deliver. To be honest, I was looking inward to Central Liverpool and to our main stakeholders rather than outwards to neighbouring PCTs. As Central Liverpool grew in strength from both its track record in delivery and influence, it became inevitable that the three PCTs would have to come together initially by integrating management under myself as Chief Executive across all three PCTs. This put us in a strong position by the time full merger of all the Boards came in October 2006. This positional power then opened the door for much stronger leadership but it had to be based, and continues to be based, on influential leadership. The two are needed for truly transformational leadership, but influence must come first.

Parallel to all of this, a change of direction was needed in the acute sector to achieve more realistic and affordable building plans. This would require a downsizing of capacity plans. This process of realisation was not an easy one for the system and, to be frank, needed a degree of courage and determination on my part. Yes, I made some mistakes along the way but that period in our history did much to build the excellent collaboration we now have in the Liverpool economy. Collaboration needs assertiveness as well as co-operation. Key to success was faith in the Model of care and the buy-in from players, and common acceptance that we could not go on as we were. This was gradually supported by the results of innovation and change achieved through joint working.

Alignment has become much more pronounced in the 2 years since the merged Liverpool PCT was formed. The benefit of one voice (and a strong voice) from the PCT and the evidence of results achieved so far have been key factors. But the main factors are of leadership, the basics of influential leadership, of collectively shaping our vision, of being a strong partner who can be relied on to deliver, of helping partners to achieve their goals and objectives both organisationally and for individuals. And of course skills of listening (and hearing), of understanding, taking the time required to move things along and developing personal and PCT gravitas whilst using our commissioning leverage, are also key learning points.

So where are we going? We have sought to be ambitious through a continuous basis of growing and re-inventing ourselves. My role is primarily one of looking ahead, to be one step ahead of the game and to enthuse Liverpool team to be responsive to change. But this is not easy. Organisations, even, or perhaps especially, those that work in the health and social care sector, sometimes have rigid territorial boundaries which are preciously guarded.

My approach has been to paint a picture for people as to how things could be. Players need to feel that they have shaped that. In some cases there was doubt that the picture was realistic or attainable. You need to show that it is possible by achieving small early steps towards it. In doing so you need to address players' current problems and issues. Only by showing how one can help them do their job and achieve their targets will you win them on board. This means appealing to Myers Briggs' preferences for individuals, e.g. detail for the Ss, appealing to beliefs for the Fs, flexibility for the Ps, etc. It also means understanding pressures and threats individuals and organisations are under – hitting targets, winning votes. We need to remember that basically everyone sets out with the intention of doing a good job. Help them do this and they will help you.

Clare Chapman, in her Guardian 2007 lecture, argued that:

"System level leadership is crucial because health is not so much an organisation but a sector, comprising hundreds of providers and partners.

We must change the whole way connections are made across the organisation as we move from being a monolithic nationalised industry to becoming a diverse, pluralist and responsive sector.

The values, culture and behaviours of the NHS can help drive this change, but only provided we properly understand and fully harness them. A greater trust across health opens the door to new relationships and a new form of accountability. Leaders need to be able to "let go", comfortable with the idea of devolving power downward, because they are confident that standards will still be met.

The trick to this lies in providing "freedom within a framework". Critical to this framework is a commitment to quality to ensure we are improving lives for patients, public and staff.

At an organisational level, leaders must ensure that the needs of the patient come ahead of the interests of the institution. A single patient can frequently require care from multiple trusts as well as both the NHS and the Social Care System. Budgets should be held in a way which works for the patient.

Within trusts we must create a shared purpose of "looking out to patients, not up at targets", which sounds easy, but isn't – as anyone who's tried bringing about this change will confirm.'

In summary then, I have learnt over the years that the role of leadership is about creating a collective vision and then to work flat out to sell that vision and make it happen. Clear communication and good team work are vital. Collaboration and partnership are key. My own personal habits are based on:

- Active listening;
- Clearing my mind of clutter;
- Thinking of the future and how to get there;
- Being myself: one of my director colleagues said to me that 'even when I think you are telling me off, I still go away feeling great';
- We all need to make change happen and working together will make it happen better;
- My view of people is to a large extent based on how I have been treated and my usual response is, 'What does that person need and how can I make it happen so that they can feel good?'

I hope you find these few thoughts helpful. We are all on a journey and mine is still not at an end. Perhaps there are doors still to be opened for me, but I must increasingly ask myself, 'Who can I open doors for?' The investment in me I need now to invest in others.

References

Chapman, C. (2008) Leading is engaging. (Speech delivered at the Guardian Public Sector Summit.) http://www.dh.gov.uk/en/Managingyourorganisation/Leadershipandmanagement/DH_083353

Details of The Myers-Briggs Type Indicator® is available at http://www.myersbriggstypeindicator.co.uk/index.htm

13

DEVELOPING DEEP EMPLOYEE ENGAGEMENT – THE BLACKPOOL WAY

Julian Hartley

T his chapter examines the challenge of developing deep employee engagement in a large acute hospital undergoing a major turnaround programme. It considers the reasons for and benefits of attempting to engage staff at a fundamental level and the leadership challenges this presents.

Background

In December 2005 I started a new job as Chief Executive of Blackpool Fylde and Wyre Hospitals NHS Trust. This was an exciting opportunity – the first time I had led an acute hospital Trust, and a job I had aspired to since being a general management trainee. The Trust I was joining appeared to be doing well – 3 star status, new capital developments and strong operational performance on key targets. However, the introduction of the new NHS funding system 'Payment by Results' (PbR) and the greater transparency it brought to Trust finances exposed a major problem. The Trust had previously used significant capital receipts to support a worsening recurrent position and although it had previously achieved financial balance the combination of PbR, new capital schemes (including a £55m Cardiac Centre) and an underlying recurrent problem led to a projected £24m deficit for the year 2006/7. This was not an uncommon situation in the NHS at that time; a number of Trusts were struggling with significant deficits and ambitious recovery programmes. Indeed it is strange in this time of accumulated surpluses to look back only two years to this period of financial 'meltdown' in the NHS when every newspaper carried more stories of NHS financial strife.

In Blackpool it was time for a deep breath and some tough decisions. This started with a sober assessment of our position by the Board employing independent accountants, following which we developed a recovery plan – one of many in the NHS at that time. This is unremarkable in itself. What was remarkable however was the size and timescale of the plan – a 10% reduction in costs on a £220m turnover within one financial year. This is an ambitious programme in any sector particularly in an organisation with little or no experience of major cost reduction and for whom the scale of our financial woes came as a real shock and was inevitably associated with the arrival of the new CEO.

However, what encouraged me was the willingness of staff to face up to the problems we had and their desire to deal with it sooner rather than later. Once we had published the scale of our financial problems and as everyone began to understand how they had arisen, there was an acknowledgement that these were best dealt with over as short a timescale as possible – a preference for an acute episode rather than a chronic one. So began the hardest year of my career to date.

Anxiety and turbulence

By the autumn of 2006, the recovery plan was in full swing. We were officially in 'turnaround', the local and regional press were all over us with headlines about cuts and job losses, we were consulting with our PCTs on the closure of two smaller but much loved local hospitals, and our staff were in a state of high anxiety. We were, however, making progress. The 'run rate' of monthly savings was picking up and we were on track to achieve our target 10% reduction in recurrent costs by the year end. However, despite the encouraging progress of our financial recovery plan, I was deeply concerned about its impact on our staff. Achieving a 10% cost reduction programme in one year meant large-scale moves of staff as we closed local hospitals and wards and hundreds of staff were redeployed to new wards and departments as vacancies were vigorously controlled and our staff numbers fell by around 500. There is no doubt that efficiency and productivity improved during this period but staff morale and well-being was badly damaged. I knew we needed to do something to tackle this and it was a corridor conversation with my Director of Estates and Facilities which started the ball rolling.

'Growing your own heroes'

Mike Gallagher, Director of Estates and Facilities, stopped me in the corridor and said, 'Julian – I've just heard the best ever presentation on managing change and getting staff on board.' Mike is a shrewd manager himself and not easily impressed, so I was interested to find out more. What Mike told me about was a presentation by John Oliver, the former Managing Director of Leyland Trucks, who had turned the company around from near oblivion to a profitable world class manufacturer. John was now leading a small team 'Team Enterprise Solutions' which was spreading the word about what he called 'deep employee engagement' which is fully described in his excellent book, *Growing Your Own Heroes.*

We asked John to come and talk to us in the Trust. He is an inspiring and thought-provoking speaker and he went down a storm in the Trust. His blend of practical advice, turnaround experience, business acumen and a systematic framework and road map for achieving deep employee engagement really connected with us at the time. We found in John someone who was passionate about high performance through a fully engaged workforce which at the time felt like the Holy Grail we were seeking. John for his part was fascinated by the NHS and by the prospect of introducing his approach within a large, busy hospital undergoing major turnaround. John agreed to work with us to develop our own version of his approach and threw himself into a period of feverish activity with virtually all staff hearing his presentation at a range of organised sessions.

The first milestone in our journey towards deep employee engagement was the diagnostic of management style in the organisation. This entailed an unflinching look at ourselves via a questionnaire to staff about the management style and culture of the Trust. This process was facilitated by John and culminated in a series of presentations to all staff about the results which were designed to signal our openness about what was wrong and our desire to change.

These sessions were often cathartic for staff and enabled everyone in the Trust to 'let off steam' about the organisation and see that we were serious about change. John's observations following these sessions included (unsurprisingly):

> 'The Trust has achieved an unprecedented level of cost reduction over the last year. In order to restore financial stability, the Trust also needs a sustainable approach to ensuring competitiveness. There are a number of key challenges here:
>
> ■ Morale is not good throughout the Trust;
> ■ Trust in management has declined, with the Executive Team the focus of much of the opprobrium;
> ■ People feel bruised and somewhat confused after the actions of the past year or so;
> ■ "Agenda for Change" is widely perceived as contributing to low morale;
> ■ The Trust is very large and both geographically and functionally dispersed; and (most importantly)
> ■ Those involved in management are not united in either their understanding of the problem or the solution.'

The diagnosis of these challenges concentrated the minds of managers throughout the Trust and in particular the Board recognised the need to prioritise staff engagement as part of our turnaround activity. So was born 'the Blackpool Way' which crystallised the need for deep employee engagement and set out how we would go about achieving it.

The Blackpool Way

The Blackpool Way was now becoming the 'lingua franca' for the Trust, but initially it was met with some scepticism and suspicion. A central part of its development was the involvement of groups of staff to shape and develop the approach and the identification of a number of 'Blackpool Way Champions' from different parts of the Trust doing different jobs, but united in their support and belief in the Blackpool Way. So what exactly is the Blackpool Way? The following document from its time of introduction pins down its key components, all of which were developed and refined by our staff.

The Blackpool Way: What is it?

The Blackpool Way is the Trust's principal organisational development programme and will fundamentally change the way in which the organisation is run by:

- Developing a fully engaged workforce, where individuals and teams have greater influence and autonomy in driving the Trust towards best in class performance.
- Charging managers with achieving the Trust's objectives through an inspired and motivated workforce. Management success will, therefore, be measured in future not only by results, but how those results were obtained.
- Introducing a policy deployment approach where management ensures that local priorities match the overall imperatives and performance measures of the organisation.

The 'Blackpool Way' is not a complex theoretical model, but is a way of managing that is rooted in working hard with all managers on those attributes exhibited by the best. In essence it involves ensuring that all managers embrace the following:

Communication. This will involve a much more structured programme, based on:

- Meet the boss sessions at Executive Team and Divisional team level using a prescribed format
- Management by walking about being planned for maximum impact and with clear issues to discuss, not unfocused visits
- Complete revamp of existing communication systems, tested by regular feedback from the audience. This will involve more effective information sourcing, motivation, inspiration and upward flow of views and opinions
- A change in focus from numbers to discussion of issues
- Positive and constructive communication
- Focusing management attention on the more positive 80% of staff, rather than the negative 20%

Management style. Changing the way in which managers manage, so that managers listen, share and consult more and display a positive demeanour. In particular we will:

- Develop expected standards of behaviour for management towards the workforce

- Introduce a regular management-style questionnaire completed by subordinates and peers
- Use this to encourage local standards of behaviour for the 'Blackpool person'
- Ensure managers debate how to create a positive agenda
- Use the grapevine to gauge effectiveness
- Develop a greater intolerance to poor performance, better utilising the appraisal and disciplinary processes to tackle individuals

Recognition. Good work should not go unrecognised, and all staff respond to acknowledgement of their efforts. Our managers will become more effective at this through:

- The introduction of simple, non-financial, recognition routines
- Monitoring of frequency and effectiveness of recognition
- Introduction of non-financial recognition for teams
- Policing of recognition through a small recognition committee

Continuous improvement. We will use action teams and focus groups to deliver continuous improvement. This will be based on:

- Top-down direction
- Bottom-up engagement
- An effective process to link the two.

Time. Managers will be expected to carry out a ruthless cull on the average time they spend in meetings. All meetings will be reviewed by the Chairs of those meetings to ensure that meetings are necessary, have clear outcomes and are only as long as they need to be.

Our core business objectives will be broken down into departmental and team targets. These will be stretch targets, where we will encourage people to enjoy the challenge.

The Blackpool Person will be:
- Considerate
- Team-orientated
- Reliable
- Honest
- Open to change
- Conscientious
- Friendly
- Positive

- Customer-focused
- Patient-focused

and … have Initiative

The Blackpool Manager

Will demonstrate excellence in being:

- Visible and Approachable
- Accountable
- Decisive
- Facilitative
- Fair
- Professionally competent
- Pro-active
- Motivational

and similarly demonstrate excellence in:

- People skills
- Creating team spirit
- Listening and communication skills
- Having the integrity/courage to manage poor performance and the diligence to recognise and acknowledge good performance.

In addition, the Executive Team or equivalent will be:

- Visionary
- Inspirational

The descriptions of 'the Blackpool Person/Manager/Director' are used to explicitly convey the whole organisation's expectations in relation to behaviour. Framing the organisation's culture 'how we do things around here' in these terms has helped us deal with destructive behaviours. In short, there is as much importance placed on behaviours as on results. The business case for such an approach is conclusive. There is a weight of evidence demonstrating that an engaged workforce is more productive, has less sickness, has better recruitment and retention, higher morale and well being.

Some specific examples of the Blackpool Way in action include:

- Recognition days where frontline staff from a particular Division in the Trust showcase their achievements, innovations and good practice to the rest of the organisation.

- Celebrating Success Awards, an annual set piece event held at the Tower Ballroom where individual staff and teams are nominated for a range of awards both by other staff and by patients.

- Regular 'back to the floor' sessions where managers spend time working alongside front-line staff for a reasonable period. I have spent time working as both a porter and healthcare assistant.

- The 'Management Style' questionnaire which is completed by managers and senior clinicians (including Consultants) every six months. This questionnaire tests the extent to which the qualities and behaviours of the Blackpool Manager are being discharged and is sent to at least six of the managers' direct reports. The results are discussed by the manager with their line manager and the emphasis is on continuously improving the score and using the results to inform a more effective management system as appropriate.

- A major emphasis on communication which has a number of channels: team brief, bulletins, intranet, rumour board, road shows, all of which are monitored and regularly reviewed.

The impact of the Blackpool Way has been significant. The successful delivery of the ambitious recovery plan in 2006/7 enabled us to focus on embedding the Blackpool Way during 2007/8 as well as carrying forward the momentum of a successful turnaround to authorisation as a Foundation Trust in December 2007. The impact of the Blackpool Way on a range of indicators, particularly sickness, appraisal, recruitment and retention has been marked by positive feedback from a number of external bodies including Investors in People and the Heath and Safety Executive. All support the view that the vast majority of staff are aware of the Blackpool Way and that it has general support as a model for improving the performance of the Trust and the working lives of staff.

However, this is only the start of the journey and we have a long way to go before we can claim we have achieved deep employee engagement across the whole Trust. Nevertheless, the signs are positive and there is a tangible difference in levels of staff motivation and engagement across the Trust. It is a long way from the anxiety and turbulence of two years ago and we face future challenges with greater vision and purpose, confident in the ability of our staff to rise to those challenges – in the Blackpool Way.

References

Oliver, J. & Memmott, C. (2006) *Growing Your Own Heroes*. Cork: Oak Tree Press.

14

SPREADING THE WORD ABOUT LEADERSHIP

Ian Cumming, OBE

I have been involved for several years now in helping develop leadership skills in clinical staff. Whilst management training is often a huge turn-off to many clinicians, I have found that exploring leadership, followership and team dynamics is interesting and motivating to most people – if done appropriately. This chapter summarises some of the areas that we explore with clinicians during our programmes and aims to convey in a simple and accessible format what I believe leadership is all about. This chapter is based on *The Little Black Book of Leadership: Hints and Tips for Clinical Staff* published by and available from NHS North Lancashire.

My focus in this chapter is to 'think aloud' about leadership in the NHS. For me placing ladders is about leading through doing and by example. The greatest expression of placing ladders is about leaders creating leaders at all levels in the organisation in order to maximise the potential for improvement in patient care and the quality of services we commission or provide. It is about harnessing our energies and effort for the collective good of the population, our patients, our colleagues and the organisations we all work for.

Let me start with a few of the concepts that we try to convey in our work with clinical staff. It has been stated earlier in this book that published books, articles, case studies and blogs on leadership are voluminous. In my opinion, the underlying messages from this literature all points to some simple observations as follows:

- **Leadership is about people and about developing and communicating a vision**

I have a few friends who work alone. They manage their own time, their own projects and themselves and they are accountable to only themselves for their own actions (or to the people who employ them as contractors). Whilst being successful in this environment may require good self-discipline and good time management skills, it is not leadership as there are no followers!

Within the NHS this style of totally independent working is very rare. We all work in or with teams for much or all of our time. An additional complicating factor in the NHS is that teams change all the time. For example, a team member involved in running a morning theatre list may be in a totally different team in the afternoon. The basic concepts don't change though – leadership is practised or exercised within a context that requires people to interact as leaders and followers. The most important point to remember is that a leader cannot be a leader without followers.

It is through people that leadership is put into effect to create and communicate vision. In his book *Managing People is like Herding Cats*, Warren Bennis (1998) remarked that:

> 'Leaders come in every size, shape and disposition: short, tall, neat, sloppy, young, old, male and female; every leader I talked to shared at least one characteristic .. i.e. a concern with a guiding purpose, an overarching vision. They were more than goal-oriented.'

- **Leadership is about creating an environment in which everyone works towards a common goal or objective**

In healthcare there are any number of professional and non-professional staff, both within and across organisations, who are involved in delivering care to one patient. Knowing who is involved and strengthening the ties of those that are involved is vital in achieving our common goal. Bennis (1998) proposed that:

> 'leaders have a clear idea of what they want to do, personally and professionally and the strength to persist in the face of setback, even failures. They know where they are going and why.'

So, if you are a leader, when did you last ask yourself the question, 'Where are we going and why – what are we really trying to achieve?' Also, think about what kind of answers you might get were you to ask these questions to your team members.

■ **Leadership is an art that requires experience and practice to master**

The debate about whether leaders are born or created is age old. My personal view is that it is a bit of both! Charisma and personality of good leaders undoubtedly play a part, but many aspects of leadership are learned and developed. The other common debate is whether leadership is an art or science. My view here – despite being a scientist – is that leadership is an art. Learning about leadership is very much learning to ski; you can read about it in books, you can see others doing it, but it is not until you actually experience it for yourself that you really learn how to do it. Also, just like skiing, the more you do it the better you get at it – practice makes perfect. Continuing this analogy for a moment, when a novice skier hits ice or a bump in the snow, they fall over – more advanced skiers make the necessary changes to their technique to avoid falling. Leadership is just the same – experience allows certain situations to be 'recovered from' which less experience leaders would struggle with.

Leadership styles are emergent and dynamic – they need to be adapted to suit the need and situation. The rapidly changing context of healthcare requires us to constantly adopt, adapt and change to meet new demands. Bennis (1998) raises a question as to what kind of leader we will need to survive the 21st century. He proposed that we will need a leader 'who is innovative, original (that is concerned with their own personal development), who inspires trust, has a long range perspective and has their eyes on the horizon, challenges the status quo, is his or her own person and one who does the right thing.' And as he observed further, 'Leaders don't just appear out of thin air. They must be developed – nurtured in such a way that they acquire the qualities of leadership.'

On approaches

All of us when asked can identify successful leaders, some famous, others less so, some historic and others contemporary. Picking a few at random

– Nelson Mandela, Richard Branson, Winston Churchill and Jesus, whilst they could all be considered to be successful leaders in their own way, they have enormously different styles and approaches to leadership.

Successful leaders in healthcare need to be able to use different leadership styles on different occasions. Daniel Goleman and his colleagues (2000) have written extensively on Emotional Intelligence and Leadership. Goleman proposed that successful leaders are able to move seamlessly between six leadership styles as follows:

1. **Affiliative**: focuses on creating harmony and establishing emotional ties
2. **Authoritative**: persuades and mobilises others towards a vision;
3. **Coaching:** facilitates and supports the development and growth of others:
4. **Democratic**: consensus-oriented and encourages participation of all
5. **Pace setting**: sets and expects high standards
6. **Coercive**: demands immediate compliance.

An example I often use with clinicians about moving between leadership styles involves a resuscitation situation where time is critical. At the start of the resuscitation, the team leader would use an Authoritative or even Coercive style to ensure instructions are carried out appropriately and quickly. Once the resuscitation was over, the leader's style should change to a coaching style (lessons learned/how could we perform better next time?) or possibly even an affiliative style (particularly if the resuscitation was unsuccessful and/or perhaps there were some people involved in their first resuscitation).

The building blocks of placing ladders – traits of good leaders

Whoever your role model as a leader, there are certain traits that all good leaders share.

■ **Enthusiasm** – In my opinion, the most successful leaders are those that are able to convey on a consistent basis their enthusiasm for their role, their teams, their organisation and their community. Successful leaders are also almost always enthusiastic about their goals and objectives – i.e. what their teams are trying to deliver. Maintaining a motivated team is impossible if one is constantly complaining about the constant change, other leaders, lack of resources, etc. I love my job as a CEO (most of the time anyway!) and feel very privileged to work for the NHS. Unfortunately, we are not good at communicating this to others. It seems to me that the NHS is suffering from a chronic case of 'whine-itis' – this drives down morale, job satisfaction and also public perception and is something that we as leaders MUST address.

- **Commitment** – Successful leaders also need commitment – i.e. they do not give up or move on when the going gets tricky. Effective leaders also need to be interested and committed to improving their teams' performance, not just maintaining the status quo.

- **Toughness** – How many of us have worked in situations where we feel let down when those in charge avoid difficult decisions or tolerate poor performance simply to remain popular? You cannot be a good leader and always be popular! Respect is the trait successful leaders should wish to have recognised by their team – not simply popularity.

- **Fairness** – Good leaders should always treat members of their team fairly. This does not imply treating everyone the same – after all, we are all different.

- **Humility** – That we often cite Gandhi and Mandela as successful leaders is due in part to their obvious humility (or lack of arrogance if you prefer), but we also need leaders to show **confidence** in their dealings with others. Good leaders also need to be willing to take appropriate risks when warranted.

- **Integrity** – You cannot be a successful leader if no one trusts you! Integrity and trust are therefore fundamental pre-requisites amongst the traits of successful leaders.

Knowing when to place ladders

In this book we have come across numerous instances of leaders both having and relishing the opportunity of having ladders placed for them. In all the cases cited the outcome has been positive. Individuals grow when given a chance to be tested. Good leaders know when to allow this, what risks to take and when to delegate. I believe that effective leaders will never delegate anything that they are unwilling to do themselves. Delegation allows people to grow and share the load and is an effective measure as to how well the leader knows about the skills and abilities of team members.

I have found the work of Tannenbaum and Schmidt (1973) a useful framework for understanding the relationship between the amounts of freedom that a team has and the authority exerted over the team by its leader. Their ideas are best explained by the following diagram:

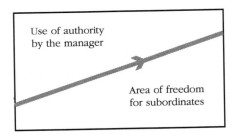

FIGURE 3: TANNENBAUM AND SCHMIDT MODEL

The model indicates that the less the authority that the leader displays over the team, the more the freedom the team members have to act. Effective leaders are able to ensure that their teams are enabled to move along the continuum on the right. High performing teams will be at the right hand end of the continuum. This is the concept of earned autonomy for teams.

Conclusions

The success of the NHS and each of us as leaders is dependent upon us having a vision with explicit goals, but also the commitment to deliver these goals. Teamwork and effective communication are key and it is vital that they become the bedrock of our everyday work. We can all make a big difference by:

- Thinking how we split our time between focusing on the task at hand, intra-team dynamics, and the needs of individuals within those teams. Are we all giving the time and effort necessary to place ladders for team members to grow?
- Reflect on how we communicate – for instance how much of our time is spent 'talking at' as opposed to 'listening to'. Remember the old adage '2 eyes, 2 ears and 1 mouth – use them in that proportion'?;
- Encouraging the giving and receiving of feedback;
- Co-creating with our teams what it is we are trying to achieve, planning how to get there and having milestones to measure progress;
- Being responsive to change and creating situations that can lead to changes that will improve the quality of care we provide;
- Having a positive attitude to the work we do;
- Remembering to thank your team for the work they do!

References

Bennis, W. (1998) *Managing People is Like Herding Cats.* London: Kogan Page.

Cumming, I. (2008) *The Little Black Book of Leadership Hints and Tips for Healthcare Staff.* Lancs: Perfect Circle.

Goleman, D. *et al.* (2000) Leadership that gets results. *Harvard Business Review* (May/June).

Tannenbaum, R. & Schmidt, W.H. (1973) How to choose a leadership pattern. *Harvard Business Review* (May/June).

15

PLACING LADDERS TO CONNECT MORE STRONGLY WITH OUR SERVICE USERS AND TEAMS

Simon Barber

A few years ago a friend of mine was shortlisted for an interview as a Policy Director in the NHS. Most of his substantial experiences were gained overseas. At the interview he was asked what he was bringing to the post which would add value given that his work and expertise was grounded overseas. His response was that, as he was not socialised in the NHS, he was bringing fresh eyes that could see different possibilities. The casting vote gave him the head nod.

Such outcomes are rare these days as experience, achievements, performance and testimony are vital in what is an ever-increasing competitive landscape. But the anecdote conjures for me a vivid image as to what placing ladders is all about. At its simplest level, it is about those who place ladders and those who are climbers. It can be seen as a two-way thing. One the one hand most, if not all, of us have had ladders placed for us; on the other we have placed ladders for others. Perhaps that's what it is all about – give and take. But there is more to it. What kind of person or leader is more inclined to place ladders for others? And on the flip side, how much of placing ladders are we as leaders doing? My hunch is that the more we place ladders, the more success we will achieve in our respective roles and organisations and I will come back to this issue later.

In my own case, I was desperately in need of some ladders to climb and perhaps on reflection, justifiably so. Most of my colleagues in this book have had long and successful track records in the NHS. In some cases their entire careers have been spent in the NHS. But I am a newcomer and only joined the NHS two years ago.

Most of my working life prior to this point was spent in the commercial sector and had I gained substantial experience as a Finance and Commercial director in Utilities, Manufacturing and Telecoms. To a greater extent my career was characterised by change and a common thread in most of my posts was that of turning around failing companies to success and then in many cases to mergers and acquisitions. After years in this sector and having re-assessed my personal values, I decided that it was time to use my skills and abilities in a different avenue.

Although on the outside of it, I was very aware of the issues, and financial issues in particular, in the NHS. On a more personal level my wife works as a nurse and my sister is an Occupational Therapist in healthcare. In part it was through this connection that I decided to explore working in the NHS as a result of re-assessing where I wanted to go with the rest of my working life.

I decided that I would test out a move into the health sector. I showed my CV to a CEO in health care who felt that it was a strong CV but that it would be difficult to break into the NHS in a permanent position. He advised that I considered an interim post.

A CEO colleague was at the time working with her team at developing their Foundation Trust application. They needed to carry out a market assessment and she asked me about my experience of evaluation and how conversant I was with work of this kind. I jumped at the opportunity and carried out the work as a consultant. It was a useful start to my journey into the NHS.

As mentioned earlier, I have had considerable experience of turnaround in the commercial sector and KPMG (the business consulting company) put my name forward as an applicant for a turnaround director for a PCT. The organisation was in financial recovery and within 18 months we were able to turn the £42 million deficit into a surplus of £1.8 million. The CEO at the PCT was fulsome in support and helped with the work I was doing and became a useful role model. Within a short space of time I was lucky enough to gain the support and mentoring of another neighbouring CEO. This provided me with the confidence to seek a chief executive post.

In December 2007, I was appointed to my first CEO post to 5 Boroughs Partnership Trust providing mental health services and the main focus then was to make the organisation financially viable and lead a change management process. The recent history was one of a high level of churn at board level with a succession of CEOs and acting CEOs. It is a complex Partnership Trust serving 4 PCTs organisations and 5 Local Authorities covering a large geographical area. One PCT was threatening to leave and move its services elsewhere. Working relationships between the organisations in some cases was poor and there was an opportunity to provide a major service improvement change programme.

Coming to a new post with a lot to do is something that really fires one's imagination and appetite for doing something that can make a difference. There is a sense of excitement – the opportunity to try and test out ideas but equally the challenge to sell a vision or an idea and to make it happen with and through others. This is true for us all irrespective of what level of the organisation we work. In my own case it may be that I had something to prove but my intention and commitment was to do something different and to help create a vision that could engage people within our organisation to deliver on service improvement.

John Kotter (2002), the business guru and thinker, has written extensively on all aspects of strategy and has commented on the importance of an effective vision. He listed a number of key elements as follows:

- **Imaginable** in that it should be able to convey an image as to what the future will look like;
- **Desirable** which means that it appeals to needs and interest of staff, service users [customers] and others who have a stake in the organisation
- **Feasible** in that it is realistic and attainable
- **Focused** in terms of being sharp and explicit in guiding decision making
- **Flexible** by which it should enable individual initiatives and the capacity to respond to changing circumstances
- **Communicable** so that it is easy to talk about and engage with.

Perhaps the greatest challenge for leaders in times of transformational change is the ability to champion the cause through a direct appeal to people and staff so as to arouse their own passion and cause to commit to the work that needs to be done. In a geographically dispersed organisation it is even more necessary to ensure that strategic leadership is obvious, effectively communicated and has an impact on the ground. Given the pressing need to achieve small wins, it was essential to harness energies and efforts in a concerted way. Kotter's framework for creating major change offers some useful insights that can be adapted to suit organisational agendas as follows:

1: need to establish a sense of urgency
2: creating a guiding coalition
3: developing a vision and strategy
4: communicating the change vision
5: empowering broad-based action
6: generating short-term wins
7: consolidating gains and producing more change
8: anchoring new approaches in the culture.

The first strategy we put in place was to reduce the organisational load of senior leaders to enable them to focus on key areas so that they can deliver on core objectives. One colleague, who for instance had the portfolio of 4 key functions, was relieved of 3 of these so that he could focus on quality. Others were promoted to key operational roles.

With a small senior team with a sharper focus in place, I then began to examine the manner in which strategic decisions were made and implemented within and across the organisation. There was nothing equivalent to a Professional Executive Committee in place. I encouraged the Medical Director to set up a Professional Advisory Group (PAG) so that clinicians could lead on the direction of strategy. To develop and deliver an effective and modern people strategy, I appointed a Director from outside the NHS with responsibility for leading on an effective Human Resource [HR] strategy and to lead on the organisation development agenda. With full board strength in place, we were able to assess and monitor what was happening and in particular to celebrate the small wins that were happening on the ground.

The role of service users in decision making in the NHS has attracted considerable attention over the past decade and will become even more pressing given the Lord Darzi Review. My own experience outside the NHS has afforded me useful insight on customer care strategies in a variety of business sectors. I believed that there were a number of useful transferable insights that could be refined and applied to the NHS. Given the underpinning social care model ethos of the NHS, I felt that it was important to develop a much tighter alignment of service user involvement and feedback at the planning, delivery and evaluation of services.

We decided to give added impetus to the championing of service users across the organisation and to bring service users' voices in a more strategic way to inform and shape service provision including making a strong commitment backed up with solid action to enable:

- service users to take part in appointment panels for staff [including my own appointment as Chief Executive];
- service users to participate in investigating serious clinical incidents;
- service user involvement that is central to our strategic and operational communication strategy;
- the piloting of a Patient Opinion website [although these were in place in a number of Acute trusts, we were the first trust to have piloted this in the Mental Health area]
- the taking of steps to bolster the amount of support for the community services so that they could respond on a more agile basis to service needs in the community.

It was also necessary that, as a management team, we created a vision that was high on aspiration and made obvious through a set of key strategic objectives, but broken down in the following terms:

Key strategic objectives
↓
Year 1 corporate objectives
↓
Objectives for every part of the service
↓
Made relevant to personal development plans
↓
Linked back to strategic objective

In effect, what we sought to do was to create a 'Golden Thread' linkage and were able to do this through whole system engagement activities. This is not rocket science and whilst elements of this were attempted in parts of the organisation previously, this was the first time that it was done across the organisation as a whole. Staff welcomed the approach as it provided a shared and common purpose. They also began to realise that they and the work that they were doing was valued.

To help sharpen the focus of the services, we also sought to develop five service streams comprising:

1. Adult services
2. Older people's services
3. Children and Young people's services
4. Forensics
5. Leaning Disabilities.

Each service stream was required to carry out regular analysis of service development needs and to propose service development strategies. These were then presented to the Trust Board and once approved were rolled out to clinical teams where ownership resided.

The main messages we sought to convey to our people were that:

- quality and service development were paramount;
- high quality will only be assured through engaging clinical and front line teams;
- that service improvement can be maximised if we can learn from each other, share good practice and work towards a supportive and enabling work environment;
- the role that service users play is central to the services we provide and that there was no part for us to tell them what they wanted;
- listening to, playing back and checking out what we understand based on service users and team feedback are invaluable to the way in which we shape and deliver our services;
- as an organisation and leadership team, we have got to listen to our staff and service users.

I have therefore made a conscious effort not to be trapped in my office. Operating in 38 different sites across five Local Authorities and five inpatient sites means that senior leaders have to be visible and accessible to be able to have conversations and to hear stories about what we can do together about making a bigger difference. Our Trust Board meetings take place in different boroughs on a rotational basis and we spend the afternoons at walkabouts and meetings with staff in those boroughs. Our Employee of the Month Award Ceremonies also provide opportunities for me to present the awards personally and to meet winners and their teams as well as other staff at those sites to strengthen involvement and engagement.

All of us who work in the health service can make a difference to the quality of service of our users and the working lives of our colleagues. Challenges and problems will arise and there will be times when we will all have to make hard and difficult choices. The overriding concern should be about raising the bar of outcomes that our work is having on our service users, the community in which we work and live in. Being receptive to the views of others and engaging them on the service improvement journey is something which has become the focus of my own placing ladders journey.

References

Kotter, J. (2002) *The Heart of Change.* Boston: HBS Publishing.

16

ON BEING POSITIVE

Mike Burrows

S ome readers may recall the book *Touching the Void* by Joe Simpson (1988). The story was subsequently made into a film of the same title. The book tells the true story of Simpson and his fellow climber Simon Yates' successful ascent up the Siula Grande, the 6344 metres-high peak in the Peruvian Andes. Simpson and Yates are accomplished professional climbers and were the first to have ascended the vertical west face of the Siula Grande.

On their way down, however, disaster struck as Simpson suffered a smashed tibia in an accident when he slipped down an ice cliff. But the accident wasn't the only setback. Due to bad weather, they had taken much longer to make the climb and as a result they had no fuel left for heating their stove [which they required to melt snow into drinking water]. They therefore needed to get back to their base camp at 3000 feet very quickly. They began the descent by attaching themselves to each end of a long rope which was joined together. Yates dug himself in a hole in the snow and began to lower Simpson down.

The tactic worked and Simpson was lowered to the point of the joined rope but was then stuck as the knot could not pass through the belay plates. To overcome this, Simpson had to stand on his good leg to afford some slack so that Yates could unclip the rope and thread it back on the other side of the knot. This was achieved but as Yates continued the lowering, Simpson suffered a second disaster. As he was passing down a 100-foot overhanging cliff, the knot became jammed against the belay plates and he was left dangling in mid-air. Yates heroically held on for an hour but could feel the weight of Simpson gradually pulling him down away from the hole in which he was secured. Fearing that Simpson was unable to secure himself and that his bucket seat was collapsing, Yates agonisingly cut the rope. Simpson fell in a crevasse.

The next morning Yates climbed down the mountain, passing the crevasse and felt certain that Simpson must have died in the fall. But Simpson on taking in the rope, realised that it was cut and managed to abseil onto an ice bridge from where he manage to crawl back onto the glacier. With fortitude and will, and surviving three days without food and water [save for sips from melting ice], Simpson managed to crawl and hopped his way back to the base camp just a few hours before Yates had intended to leave the base camp.

Some of the stories in this book focus on issues about leadership ranging from passion, authenticity, ambition and commitment amongst others. The aspect that I have chosen to write about is being positive which for me is perhaps one of the key attitudes to have as a leader.

Firstly I was trained as a research biochemist and, as you would guess, working as a bench scientist can sometimes be a very solitary task. I was determined to see my programme of research through and made up my mind at a very early stage of my career that I was going to cast my net elsewhere from medical biochemistry. My reasons were twofold.

Firstly I wanted to work in an environment where there was more social interaction with people. And secondly, and perhaps more importantly, I believed in the NHS and its founding principles. It was a tough choice to turn my back on the science I was so passionate about but I always felt there was a contribution I could make in another area. Having left the solitary world of a bench scientist, I joined the NHS in 1986 as a trainee accountant as part of the Financial Management Training Scheme. From then to even now I constantly have to point out to others that, yes, I am a real doctor [having gained a doctorate in medical biochemistry] but I am not a medical doctor.

The other curious point about my background in the NHS is that for the most part of my early to mid-career gained in 5–6 organisations, every organisation that I have ever worked in no longer exists. I'm not sure if it was something I did! Yes, they have disappeared through closure, mergers or restructuring. Indeed my first significant post at Director level was specifically as a Finance Director working on the closure and smooth transfer of functions to successor organisations. For some these are not the kind of formative experiences that lend themselves to the making of a positive being. But they are for me, and indeed have caused me to become even more so. In a curious kind of way it was because of my positive attitude and approach during the year of this particular post that I attracted some significant attention that led to my career growth at chief executive level. And I will say more on this later.

As we have seen in other accounts in this book, placing ladders is a two-way game; it has give and take dimensions and for now I would like to highlight the positive experiences of the people who have placed ladders for me. I have always believed that we have much to learn from role models and one of the defining qualities of those that have opened doors for me is that they have all been excellent role models. The first of these was a Finance Director who first took me under his wing, so to speak. He was a tremendous mentor, a wise man and I learnt a lot from his wisdom. He was one of the first people to have ensured that I not only had wide exposure to the range of financial work experience within the organisation, but he recognised the value of me having contact, interaction and exposure to a wide array of clinical departments and colleagues outside of the Finance Dept. Of these, my time being scrubbed up in theatre and learning about the work of colleagues in this speciality was a gut wrenching [in more ways than one] experience. It brought to the fore in my mind the multiple considerations that have to be made in the clinical management of cases and of the value and need for closer working relationships between managers and clinicians.

The other key experience gained from this mentor was the involvement of board level work which required me to work on a set of challenging issues relating to the closure of beds in the locality. Many of us can recall and still see the emotive headlines in press coverage regarding service and organisational restructuring, especially relating to hospital closures and removal of key services elsewhere. I quickly appreciated and came to terms with the importance of how to carry the public and other partners with one in respect of major service change. But it was equally informative to see the people skills of an effective leader who was a role model on change management.

In another now extant Health Authority, I had the opportunity to work with an Assistant Director of Finance who foremost of all believed in me.

He was a fantastic role model – thorough and dedicated. He sometimes took risks at throwing me in at the deep end but I knew I could always turn to him for support. It also made me want to do and perform well for him which resulted in more and more doors being opened. At other Health Authority posts I was struck by the sheer passion and integrity with which colleagues carried out their work. These were tremendous learning opportunities and gave me a great deal to emulate.

In one of my first posts within an Acute Trust, I had the privileged of working with an amazing Chief Executive. She had a wonderful way with people and was caring and ambitious. She gave me a great deal of insight of working with clinicians and particularly in the area of breaking down barriers between managers and clinicians that so often gets in the way of making things happen. She exercised a great deal of trust and confidence in others. She also had a lot of faith in colleagues to make decisions and to exercise leadership in taking forward those ideas and decisions.

Far too often we see leaders who are quick to jump in and decide for others. I have learnt a lot from this colleague and have tried to develop my own ability about having and providing faith in others to give of their best. But I have also learnt that giving people the freedom to make decisions also carries with it the responsibility that they have the tools and authority to carry out their role. Learning to see the world through others' perspective and viewpoint makes us wiser and more enabling in our interactions with them.

What these experiences have taught me is that the NHS has a great many people who are concerned about making a difference; who behave with integrity and trust and who are keen to support others; who value the development of others and make time and effort to help bring this about. I am also aware, however, that this is not the experience of all who work in the NHS and we all have more work to do to make it so.

The build up to my first substantive post at director level was through a short spell at the then North West Regional Office. I was engaged in a small number of projects that provided much exposure to a range of experiences involving the wider political environment including involvement with the Department of Health. Perhaps, to coin Donald Rumsfeld's phrase, it gave me a real awareness of 'the unknown unknowns'. This experience enabled me to apply for my first substantive post at director level. My main responsibility was to manage the closure of an organisation and I saw this as a major challenge at effecting the smooth transfer to the successor organisations.

Many colleagues up and down the country would have experienced going to work but feeling uncertain about their future. I saw my role as one of providing as much assurance as possible and to keep my staff motivated so that they could deliver good care. I was also in a similar boat. I had no post to go to and it was possible that I may have had to apply for a more junior post, but I was determined to do a good job and to do it well. What I learnt here most of all is about the importance of teamwork and of the value of investing in teams to perform well.

The work I did at enabling the smooth transfer of functions to the successor organisations did get me noticed and I was appointed to a Director of Finance and then subsequently to a CEO post within Salford PCT. The top team here, and particularly the CEO and Chairman, were a dynamic combination and from them I learnt a lot about how to set standards high and to deliver best quality services. The formula consisted of:

- Recruiting able people
- Getting the right people in role
- Nurture dynamic work relationships
- Investing in people strategy.

Learning was fostered from the executive team to the front line. Personally I have always found it easy to learn and am always learning, but in a Teaching PCT learning is important for all staff to deliver a shared vision. A number of theorists including Peter Senge (1990), Mike Pedler (1991) and Watkins & Marsick (1992) have promoted the concept of the Learning Organisation. Whilst there is still a healthy debate about the elusiveness of Learning Organisations in practice, it is clear that there has been considerable attempt and commitment at working towards an organisation that reflects key elements as described below:

'A Learning Organisation is one in which people are continually encouraged and supported to increase their capacity to create results they desire, where thinking and learning are nurtured and where people are learning to see the whole together.' (Senge 1990)

'A Learning Company is a vision of what might be possible ... it can only happen as a result of learning at the whole organisational level and one that facilitates learning of all its members so as to continuously transform itself.' (Pedler *et al.* 1991)

'Learning organisations are developed through total employee engagement, collaborative learning and collective accountability towards shared values or principles.' (Watkins & Marsick 1992)

As Sandra Kerka (1995) has suggested, 'Learning is valuable, continuous, and most effective when shared and that every experience is an opportunity to learn.' Organisations should strive to provide:

- continuous learning opportunities.
- situations where employees are encouraged to use learning to reach their goals.
- a tight fit between individual performance with organisational performance.
- a culture to foster inquiry and dialogue, making it safe for people to share openly and take risks.
- a willingness to embrace creative tension as a source of energy and renewal.

The opportunities facing PCTs in terms of Fit For Purpose, World Class Commissioning and Arm's Length Provider Organisations amongst other organisational priorities, provide enormous opportunities for collaborative learning. Some of this will need to be driven top-down but in essence it is vital that this is effectively communicated and engaged with front line-up. Moreover, the value of nurturing learning and shared understanding within the organisation is also equally important for cross boundary and partnership working. And I was fortunate to have had the privilege of working and learning with a Social Services Director at district level who was passionate about how social care could improve and transform individual lives. She had the ability to take the perspective of how senior level decisions would affect individual service users and this taught me a lot regarding the importance of ensuring this is a dimension in all aspects of the decisions we take.

So what have we been focusing on to deliver quality services here at Salford Teaching PCT?

1. Firstly we have placed considerable importance to team development which is a key part to an organisational approach at matching people to roles.

2. We have put in motion a talent management programme which is being developed jointly with Salford University at identifying and matching people from the key services for managerial roles. This is being driven by a customised curriculum for junior and middle managers working with a modular programme that comprise modules including:
   – People management
   – Project management
   – Technical roles.

3. Creating opportunities for individuals to learn externally, through networks, regional engagements and secondments.

4. Fostering collaborative working with Local Authorities through Partnerships Boards.

5. Developing closer formal and informal links with service users and carers.

6. Evaluating everything we do.

And so back to the Simpson story. Whilst a vivid and powerful example of the power of hope and the will to survive, albeit in a perilous and life threatening situation, all of us have to face up to challenges of different sorts in our working lives. And we have a choice. We can choose to see the positive and grow from it or we can choose to see the negative with its energy sapping consequences. The American Psychologist, David Cooperrider (1990), who has done much to popularise the strength-based approach to change known as Appreciative Inquiry (AI), has suggested,

> 'that every organisation has something that works right- things that give it life when it is most alive, effective, successful, and connected in healthy ways to its stakeholders and communities. AI begins by identifying what

is positive and connecting it in ways that heighten energy and vision for change.'

'AI is important because it works to bring the whole organisation together to build upon its positive core. AI encourages people to work together, to promote a better understanding of the human system, the heartbeat of the organisation.'

As leaders, we have a crucial role in:

- Appreciating and valuing the best of *what is*;
- Envisioning what *can be*;
- Having conversations about what *should be*; and
- Helping to innovate for what *will be*.

References

Cooperrider, D. (1990) Positive image, positive action: the affirmative basis of organising. In: Srivastva, S. & Cooperrider, D. (eds) *Appreciative Management and Leadership: The Power of Positive Thought and Action in Organisations.* San Francisco: Jossey-Bass.

Kerka, S. (1995) The learning organization: myths and realities. Eric Clearinghouse, http://www.cete.org/acve/docgen.asp?tbl=archive&ID=A028.

Pedler, M., Burgoyne, J. & Boydell, T. (1991, 1996) *The Learning Company. A Strategy for Sustainable Development.* London: McGraw-Hill.

Senge, P.M. (1990) *The Fifth Discipline. The Art and Practice of the Learning Organization.* London: Random House.

Simpson, J. (1988) *Touching the Void.* London: Vintage.

Watkins, K. & Marsick, V. (1992) Building the learning organization: a new role for human resource developers. *Studies in Continuing Education,* Vol 14, No 2, pp. 115–129.